Supernatural Living

Through the
Gifts of the Holy Spirit

by
A.L. and Joyce Gill

ISBN 0-941975-34-7

Powerhouse Publishing
P.O. Box 99
Fawnskin, CA 92333
(909) 866-3119

Books By A.L. and Joyce Gill

God's Promises for Your Every Need
Destined for Dominion
Out! In the Name of Jesus
Victory over Deception!

Manuals in This Series

Authority of the Believer
How to Quit Losing And
Start Winning

The Church Triumphant
Through the Book of Acts

God's Provision for Healing
Receiving and Ministering
God's Healing Power

The Ministry Gifts
Apostle, Prophet, Evangelist,
Pastor, Teacher

Miracle Evangelism
God's Plan to Reach the World

New Creation Image
Knowing Who You Are in Christ

Patterns for Living
From the Old Testament

Praise and Worship
Becoming Worshipers of God

Acknowledgments
It is with great appreciation that we acknowledge
the contribution of John Decker and Lin Rang for their many hours
of work on this manual. Their suggestions and additions to this work
have contributed greatly to its completion.

About The Authors

A.L. and Joyce Gill are internationally known speakers, authors and Bible teachers. A.L.'s apostolic ministry travels have taken him to over fifty nations of the world, preaching to crowds exceeding one hundred thousand in person and to many millions by radio and television.

Their top-selling books and manuals have sold over two million copies in the United States. Their writings, which have been translated into many languages, are being used in Bible schools and seminars around the world.

The powerful life-changing truths of God's Word explode in the lives of others through their dynamic preaching, teaching, writing and video and audio tape ministry.

The awesome glory of the presence of God is experienced in their praise and worship seminars as believers discover how to become true and intimate worshipers of God. Many have discovered a new and exciting dimension of victory and boldness through their teachings on the authority of the believer.

The Gills have trained many believers to step into their own God-given supernatural ministries with the healing power of God flowing through their hands. Many have learned to be supernaturally natural as they are released to operate in all nine gifts of the Holy Spirit in their daily lives and ministries.

Both A.L. and Joyce have Master of Theological Studies degrees. A.L. has also earned a Doctor of Philosophy in Theology degree from Vision Christian University. Their ministry is solidly based on the Word of God, is centered on Jesus, strong in faith and taught in the power of the Holy Spirit.

Their ministry is a demonstration of the Father's heart of love. Their preaching and teaching are accompanied by powerful anointing, signs, wonders, and healing miracles with many being slain in waves under the power of God.

Signs of revival including waves of holy laughter, weeping before the Lord and awesome manifestations of God's glory and power are being experienced by many who attend their meetings.

A Word To Teachers And Students

Through this powerful and practical study, believers will be released into operating in all nine gifts of the Holy Spirit. From an intimate relationship with the Holy Spirit each person will discover the joy of walking in the supernatural on a daily basis. All of the vocal, revelation and power gifts will be clearly understood and experienced.

We suggest that before teaching this course you watch or listen to the video or audio tapes on this series. The more you saturate yourself with the truths of God's Word concerning the gifts of the Holy Spirit, the more that these gifts will be stirred up to operate in your life. This manual will then provide the outline for you to use while you impart these truths to others and release them into **Supernatural Living.**

Personal life illustrations are a must for effective teaching. The author has omitted these from this work so that the teacher will provide illustrations from his or her own rich experiences, or those of others to which the students will be able to relate. It should always be remembered that it is the Holy Spirit who has come to teach us all things, and that when we are studying or when we are teaching we should always be empowered and led by the Holy Spirit.

It is also important to take time at the end of each lesson for each believer to "step out of the boat" and operate in each of these gifts while they're studied. It is recommended that each lesson is followed by a short time of praise and worship. Next, encourage each one to step out by faith and release the gift, which has just been studied, to flow through them. After a period of allowing the gifts to flow in the whole group, it is suggested that you have them break up into smaller groups with leaders who have been instructed ahead of time to encourage each one to experience these gifts operating in their life.

This study is excellent for personal or group studies, Bible schools, Sunday schools, and home groups. It is important that both the teacher and the student have copies of this manual in hand during the course of the study.

The best books are written in, underlined, meditated upon and digested. Each student should therefore have their own manual. We have left space for your notes and comments. The format has been designed with a fast reference system for review and to assist you in finding areas again. The special format makes it possible for each person, once they have studied through this material, to teach the contents to others.

Paul wrote to Timothy:

> **And the things that you have heard from me among many witnesses, commit these to faithful men who will be able to teach others also. 2 Timothy 2:2**

This course is designed as a practical participation Bible course in the MINDS (Ministry Development System) format which is a specially developed approach to programmed learning. This concept is designed for multiplication in the lives, the ministry and the future teaching of the students. Former students, by using this manual, can teach this course easily to others.

Table Of Contents

The Holy Spirit

Who Is Holy Spirit?

If we are to really know God, we must not only know the Father and the Son, but we must also know the Holy Spirit in a real and personal way.

God is one in essence, yet is identified in three distinct and individual Persons. Each Person of the Godhead is equal and each shares in all of the attributes of God. Each Person of the Godhead, as revealed separately, has a definite function and personality. The Holy Spirit, just as the Father and the Son, desires for us to come into a personal relationship with Him. He wants us to live and walk intimately united with Him, recognizing the importance of His function in our daily lives.

FUNCTION OF HOLY SPIRIT REVEALED IN OLD TESTAMENT

At Creation

The Holy Spirit was part of the Trinity at creation.

Genesis 1:1-3 In the beginning God created the heavens and the earth. The earth was without form, and void; and darkness was on the face of the deep. And the Spirit of God was hovering over the face of the waters.

The "Spirit of God" was a wind, breath, blast, tempest, a whirlwind.

Psalms 104:30 You send forth Your Spirit, they are created; and You renew the face of the earth.

Interaction with Men

➤ *Came Upon*

During the period of the Old Testament, the Holy Spirit didn't dwell in men. He came upon them to anoint them for a special act or service.

I Samuel 10:6 Then the Spirit of the LORD will come upon you, and you will prophesy with them and be turned into another man.

➤ *Given Wisdom*

Exodus 28:3a So you shall speak to all who are gifted artisans, whom I have filled with the spirit of wisdom.

➤ *Strives With*

Genesis 6:3a And the LORD said, "My Spirit shall not strive with man forever ... "

➢ *Spoke To*

> **Ezekiel 2:2 Then the Spirit entered me when He spoke to me, and set me on my feet; and I heard Him who spoke to me.**

FUNCTION OF HOLY SPIRIT REVEALED IN GOSPELS

During the life of Christ, the Holy Spirit still came upon men and women for a special function, but following Christ's return to heaven and the day of Pentecost, He came to abide within men and women.

John the Baptist

> **Luke 1:15 For he will be great in the sight of the Lord, and shall drink neither wine nor strong drink. He will also be filled with the Holy Spirit, even from his mother's womb.**

Elizabeth

> **Luke 1:41 And it happened, when Elizabeth heard the greeting of Mary, that the babe leaped in her womb; and Elizabeth was filled with the Holy Spirit.**

Zechariah

> **Luke 1:67 Now his father Zacharias was filled with the Holy Spirit, and prophesied ...**

FUNCTION OF HOLY SPIRIT IN LIFE AND MINISTRY OF JESUS

Jesus Conceived by Spirit

> **Matthew 1:20,24 But while he thought about these things, behold, an angel of the Lord appeared to him in a dream, saying, "Joseph, son of David, do not be afraid to take to you Mary your wife, for that which is conceived in her is of the Holy Spirit."**

Jesus by His virgin birth, was totally a man yet He was also totally and completely God. His becoming a man had in no way diminished His essence and character as God.

Jesus Gave up Rights

Jesus willfully laid aside all of His rights and privileges as God while He was alive on this earth. He had come as the "last Adam" to fulfill all that He had created man to do on this earth when He created the first Adam.

> **Philippians 2:5-8 Let this mind be in you which was also in Christ Jesus, Who, being in the form of God, did not consider it robbery to be equal with God, but made Himself of no reputation, taking the form of a servant, and coming in the likeness of men. And being found in appearance as a man, He humbled Himself and became obedient to the point of death, even the death of the cross.**

Jesus Anointed by Spirit

Jesus' ministry didn't begin until He was baptized in water and the Holy Spirit came to empower Him and dwell within Him. Everything which Jesus did in His life and ministry from that time forward, He did as a man empowered by the Holy Spirit. This was His plan and pattern for mankind when He created them.

Matthew 3:16,17 Then Jesus, when He had been baptized, came up immediately from the water; and behold, the heavens were opened to Him, and He saw the Spirit of God descending like a dove and alighting upon Him. And suddenly a voice came from heaven, saying, "This is My beloved Son, in whom I am well pleased."

Mark 1:10 And immediately, coming up from the water, He saw the heavens parting and the Spirit descending upon Him like a dove.

➤ *Led by Spirit*

By studying the work of the Holy Spirit in the life and ministry of Jesus, we can understand the work of the Holy Spirit in our lives and ministry today. Jesus is truly our example.

Matthew 4:1 Then Jesus was led up by the Spirit into the wilderness to be tempted by the devil.

Mark 1:12 And immediately the Spirit drove Him into the wilderness.

Luke 4:1 Then Jesus, being filled with the Holy Spirit, returned from the Jordan and was led by the Spirit into the wilderness ...

➤ *Taught by Spirit*

Acts 1:2 Until the day in which He was taken up, after He through the Holy Spirit had given commandments to the apostles whom He had chosen ...

John 14:10 Do you not believe that I am in the Father, and the Father in Me? The words that I speak to you I do not speak on My own authority; but the Father who dwells in Me does the works.

➤ *Anointed by Spirit*

Luke 4:18 The Spirit of the Lord is upon Me, because He has anointed Me to preach the gospel to the poor. He has sent Me to heal the brokenhearted, to preach deliverance to the captives and recovery of sight to the blind, to set at liberty those who are oppressed.

➤ *Cast Out Demons by Spirit*

Matthew 12:28 But if I cast out demons by the Spirit of God, surely the kingdom of God has come upon you.

➤ *Offered Through Spirit*

Hebrews 9:14 How much more shall the blood of Christ, who through the eternal Spirit offered Himself without spot to God, purge your conscience from dead works to serve the living God?

➤ *Resurrected by Spirit*

Romans 1:4 And declared to be the Son of God with power, according to the Spirit of holiness, by the resurrection from the dead ...

Romans 8:11 But if the Spirit of Him who raised Jesus from the dead dwells in you, He who raised Christ from the dead will also give life to your mortal bodies through His Spirit who dwells in you.

HOLY SPIRIT IS THE POWER OF GOD

As Jesus needed the power of the Holy Spirit in His life, even so we must receive the same power of the Holy Spirit in full in our lives today!

Resurrection Power

Ephesians 1:19,20 And what is the exceeding greatness of His power toward us who believe, according to the working of His mighty power which He worked in Christ when He raised Him from the dead and seated Him at His right hand in the heavenly places ...

Power in Paul

1 Corinthians 2:4,5 And my speech and my preaching were not with persuasive words of human wisdom, but in demonstration of the Spirit and of power, that your faith should not be in the wisdom of men but in the power of God.

Romans 15:17-19 Therefore I have reason to glory in Christ Jesus in the things which pertain to God. For I will not dare to speak of any of those things which Christ has not accomplished through me, in word and deed, to make the Gentiles obedient–in mighty signs and wonders, by the power of the Spirit of God, so that from Jerusalem and round about to Illyricum I have fully preached the gospel of Christ.

QUESTIONS FOR REVIEW

1. Write, in your own words, who the Holy Spirit is.

2. How did Jesus function while He lived on this earth following His water baptism and the Holy Spirit coming to live in Him?

3. How are we to function today?

Receiving Power of Holy Spirit

First Promised

> Joel 2:28,29 And it shall come to pass afterward that I will pour out My Spirit on all flesh; your sons and your daughters shall prophesy, your old men shall dream dreams, your young men shall see visions; and also on My menservants and on My maidservants I will pour out My Spirit in those days.

> Isaiah 28:11,12 For with stammering lips and another tongue He will speak to this people, to whom He said, "This is the rest with which you may cause the weary to rest," and, "This is the refreshing"; yet they would not hear.

PROMISED IN NEW TESTAMENT

By Jesus

> ➤ *Power from on High*

> Luke 24:49 Behold, I send the Promise of My Father upon you; but tarry in the city of Jerusalem until you are endued with power from on high.

> ➤ *With Holy Spirit and Fire*

> Matthew 3:11 I indeed baptize you with water unto repentance, but He who is coming after me is mightier than I, whose sandals I am not worthy to carry. He will baptize you with the Holy Spirit and fire.

> ➤ *A Good Gift*

> Luke 11:9-13 And I say to you, ask, and it will be given to you; seek, and you will find; knock, and it will be opened to you. For everyone who asks receives, and he who seeks finds, and to him who knocks it will be opened.

> If a son asks for bread from any father among you, will he give him a stone? Or if he asks for a fish, will he give him a serpent instead of a fish? Or if he asks for an egg, will he offer him a scorpion?

> If you then, being evil, know how to give good gifts to your children, how much more will your heavenly Father give the Holy Spirit to those who ask Him!

> ➤ *Rivers of Living Water*

> John 7:37-39 On the last day, that great day of the feast, Jesus stood and cried out, saying, "If anyone thirsts, let him come to Me and drink. He who believes in Me, as the Scripture has said, out of his heart will flow rivers of living water." But this He spoke concerning the Spirit, whom those believing in Him would re-

ceive; for the Holy Spirit was not yet given, because Jesus was not yet glorified.

By Peter

Acts 2:38,39 Then Peter said to them, "Repent, and let every one of you be baptized in the name of Jesus Christ for the remission of sins; and you shall receive the gift of the Holy Spirit. For the promise is to you and to your children, and to all who are afar off, as many as the Lord our God will call."

WHO IS THE BAPTIZER?

There has often been confusion in understanding the difference between the work of the Holy Spirit in baptizing every believer into the body of Jesus Christ at the moment of salvation and the work of Jesus in baptizing believers "in" or "with" the Holy Spirit.

Baptism Defined

The word "baptize" instead of being translated into our language has been transliterated into a word which sounds like the original Greek word which was used by the writers. Actually, it means "to totally identify by submersion." When a garment is dyed, it becomes totally identified with the color of the dye. It is baptized into that color.

The Holy Spirit totally identified us with Jesus Christ at the moment of salvation. Water baptism, which is commanded by God for every believer is a picture or a testimony before men that we have already been identified with Jesus in His death, burial and resurrection. However, when Jesus baptizes us in the Holy Spirit, we also become totally identified with the Holy Spirit. We receive the power of the Holy Spirit in our lives.

Holy Spirit as Baptizer

At the moment of salvation, the Holy Spirit baptizes every believer into Jesus Christ. We become intimately united with Jesus. We become members of His body.

Romans 6:3 Or do you not know that as many of us as were baptized into Christ Jesus were baptized into His death?

Galatians 3:27 For as many of you as were baptized into Christ have put on Christ.

1 Corinthians 12:13 For by one Spirit we were all baptized into one body–whether Jews or Greeks, whether slaves or free–and have all been made to drink into one Spirit.

Ephesians 5:30 For we are members of His body, of His flesh and of His bones.

Jesus as Baptizer

As a separate and distinct function and experience, the scriptures makes it clear that Jesus wants to baptize us with the Holy Spirit.

Prophesied by John

Luke 3:16 John answered, saying to them all, "I indeed baptize you with water; but One mightier than I is coming, whose sandal strap I am not worthy to loose. He will baptize you with the Holy Spirit and with fire."

Commanded by Jesus

Acts 1:4,5 And being assembled together with them, He commanded them not to depart from Jerusalem, but to wait for the Promise of the Father, "which," He said, "you have heard from Me; for John truly baptized with water, but you shall be baptized with the Holy Spirit not many days from now."

Acts 1:8 "But you shall receive power when the Holy Spirit has come upon you; and you shall be witnesses to Me in Jerusalem, and in all Judea and Samaria, and to the end of the earth."

Promised by Peter

Acts 2:38 Then Peter said to them, "Repent, and let every one of you be baptized in the name of Jesus Christ for the remission of sins; and you shall receive the gift of the Holy Spirit."

THE PROMISE RECEIVED

By Jews on Pentecost

Acts 2:1-4 Now when the Day of Pentecost had fully come, they were all with one accord in one place. And suddenly there came a sound from heaven, as of a rushing mighty wind, and it filled the whole house where they were sitting. Then there appeared to them divided tongues, as of fire, and one sat upon each of them. And they were all filled with the Holy Spirit and began to speak with other tongues, as the Spirit gave them utterance.

Acts 2:15,16 For these are not drunk, as you suppose, since it is only the third hour of the day. But this is what was spoken by the prophet Joel ...

There has been teaching that this was a one-time event. However, after the Holy Spirit came on believers in the upper room, after the lame man was healed at the gate called Beautiful, after Ananias and Sapphira died, after the deacons were chosen, after Stephen was stoned and the persecution became more pronounced, there is another recording of believers being baptized with the Holy Spirit.

By Gentiles in Samaria

Philip went to the Samaritans and revival broke out. Samaria received the word of God and then Peter and John came.

Acts 8:14-17 Now when the apostles who were at Jerusalem heard that Samaria had received the word of God, they sent Peter and John to them, who, when they had come down, prayed for them that they might receive the Holy Spirit. For as yet He had fallen upon none of them. They had only been baptized in the name of the Lord Jesus. Then they laid hands on them, and they received the Holy Spirit.

By Gentiles in Caesarea

So that we will not think the Holy Spirit came on the Jews as a one-time event, and then on the Gentiles as a one-time event, we are given the account of the believers in Caesarea.

Acts 10:44-46a While Peter was still speaking these words, the Holy Spirit fell upon all those who heard the word. And those of the circumcision who believed were astonished, as many as came with Peter, because the gift of the Holy Spirit had been poured out on the Gentiles also. For they heard them speak with tongues and magnify God.

Acts 11:15 And as I began to speak, the Holy Spirit fell upon them, as upon us at the beginning.

By Gentiles in Ephesus

The first baptism in the Holy Spirit took place about 33 A.D.(Ussher's date). Toward the end of the book of Acts, about 54 A.D., Paul came to Ephesus.

Acts 19:2-6 He said to them, "Did you receive the Holy Spirit when you believed?"

And they said to him, "We have not so much as heard whether there is a Holy Spirit."

And he said to them, "Into what then were you baptized?"

So they said, "Into John's baptism."

Then Paul said, "John indeed baptized with a baptism of repentance, saying to the people that they should believe on Him who would come after him, that is, on Christ Jesus."

When they heard this, they were baptized in the name of the Lord Jesus. And when Paul had laid hands on them, the Holy Spirit came upon them, and they spoke with tongues and prophesied.

PAUL'S TEACHING ON HOLY SPIRIT

Did You Receive?

Acts 19:2a He said to them, "Did you receive the Holy Spirit when you believed?"

This was the first question Paul asked the believers when they arrived in Ephesus. He knew that every believer needed the power of the Holy Spirit to be an effective witness.

Their reply was typical of many Christians today.

Acts 19:2b,6 "We have not so much as heard whether there is a Holy Spirit."

And when Paul had laid hands on them, the Holy Spirit came upon them, and they spoke with tongues and prophesied.

This was the beginning of the greatest evangelistic outreach in all the history of the province of Asia! The result of believers having the power of the baptism of the Holy Spirit in their lives was the beginning of a great wave of miracle evangelism.

Acts 19:10 And this continued for two years, so that all who dwelt in Asia heard the word of the Lord Jesus, both Jews and Greeks.

RECEIVING HOLY SPIRIT TODAY

For Everyone

Jesus said we would receive power when the Holy Spirit came.

Acts 1:8a "But you shall receive power when the Holy Spirit has come upon you ..."

Peter said that everyone would receive the gift of the Holy Spirit.

Acts 2:38 Then Peter said to them, "Repent, and let every one of you be baptized in the name of Jesus Christ for the remission of sins; and you shall receive the gift of the Holy Spirit."

A Good Gift

We should desire every good gift that the Father has for us.

Luke 11:11-13 If a son asks for bread from any father among you, will he give him a stone? Or if he asks for a fish, will he give him a serpent instead of a fish? Or if he asks for an egg, will he offer him a scorpion? If you then, being evil, know how to give good gifts to your children, how much more will your heavenly Father give the Holy Spirit to those who ask Him!

To receive the gift of the Holy Spirit we are to simply ask for it, and then receive it by faith.

QUESTIONS FOR REVIEW

1. When Jesus talked about the coming of the Holy Spirit what descriptive words did He use?

2. How does one receive the baptism in the Holy Spirit according to the Word of God?

3. Explain the difference between the baptism "of" the Holy Spirit and the baptism "in" or "with" the Holy Spirit.

4. What manifestation was recorded in the New Testament as the evidence that usually followed the experience of receiving the baptism in the Holy Spirit?

Speaking in Tongues

Don't Forbid

Isn't it strange that the only gift of the Holy Spirit we are told not to forbid, is forbidden by so many groups today? It is as though Paul never wrote,

1 Corinthians 14:39 Therefore, brethren, desire earnestly to prophesy, and do not forbid to speak with tongues.

Why is there so much controversy concerning the gift of tongues? How can any gift of the Holy Spirit be so rejected and despised?

Could it be that the gift of tongues is our spirit praying directly to God – our spirit giving Him praise – our mind being renewed just as the apostle Paul said?

Of course, Satan would try to stop anything this powerful. The gift of tongues is the evidence of a person having received the baptism in the Holy Spirit. It is the doorway to living in the supernatural realm that is open for every believer.

EVIDENCE OF RECEIVING BAPTISM IN HOLY SPIRIT

On Day of Pentecost

When believers receive the baptism in the Holy Spirit and are thereby filled with the Holy Spirit, they begin to speak in tongues supernaturally as the Spirit gives the vocal inspiration. This is what happened on the Day of Pentecost.

Acts 2:4 And they were all filled with the Holy Spirit and began to speak with other tongues, as the Spirit gave them utterance.

Gentiles at Caesarea

Often, when the revelation of God's power through the Holy Spirit is shared with people, the anointing is so great that the Holy Spirit "falls" upon them and they begin to speak in tongues and magnify God.

Acts 10:44-46a While Peter was still speaking these words, the Holy Spirit fell upon all those who heard the word. And those of the circumcision who believed were astonished, as many as came with Peter, because the gift of the Holy Spirit had been poured out on the Gentiles also. For they heard them speak with tongues and magnify God.

Paul at Ephesus

Many times people receive the baptism of the Holy Spirit when the hands of a Spirit-baptized believer are laid upon them. Often, they not only begin to speak with tongues but the other gifts of the Holy Spirit are immediately activated in their lives.

Acts 19:2,6 He said to them, "Did you receive the Holy Spirit when you believed?"

And they said to him, "We have not so much as heard whether there is a Holy Spirit."

And when Paul had laid hands on them, the Holy Spirit came upon them, and they spoke with tongues and prophesied.

Paul Spoke in Tongues

Paul was thankful and realized the importance of speaking in tongues often and for long periods of time. If the apostle Paul needed to speak often in tongues, how much more do we need the same in our lives today?

1 Corinthians 14:18 I thank my God I speak with tongues more than you all ...

Two Basic Tongues

➤ *Of Men and of Angels*

When we speak with the tongues of men, we speak in one of the languages of this world. But Paul also said that he spoke in a language which the angels speak, a heavenly language.

1 Corinthians 13:1a Though I speak with the tongues of men and of angels ...

Often when expressing our love to God during our personal times of praise and worship, we run out of words in our human language to express our hearts to God. After receiving the baptism of the Holy Spirit, we can, like Paul, begin to speak in a new heavenly language, a language without the limitations of our vocabulary, the same language that the angels are worshiping God with, day and night before the throne.

WHAT HAPPENS WHEN WE SPEAK IN TONGUES?

Our Spirit Prays

When we pray in tongues, our spirit is praying by a supernatural manifestation of the Holy Spirit. Our mind is unfruitful.

1 Corinthians 14:14 For if I pray in a tongue, my spirit prays, but my understanding is unfruitful.

Declares Works of God

When Spirit-baptized believers speak in tongues, they're bringing praise to God by speaking of His wonderful works.

Acts 2:11 Cretans and Arabs-we hear them speaking in our own tongues the wonderful works of God.

Spirit Intercedes

While praying in tongues, the thoughts don't come from my mind, nor are they limited to my own understanding. Instead the Holy Spirit is praying through my human spirit directly to the Father.

Ephesians 6:18 Praying always with all prayer and supplication in the Spirit, being watchful to this end with all perseverance and supplication for all the saints.

Romans 8:26,27 Likewise the Spirit also helps in our weaknesses. For we do not know what we should pray for as we ought, but the Spirit Himself makes intercession for us with groanings which cannot be uttered. Now He who searches the hearts knows what the mind of the Spirit is, because He makes intercession for the saints according to the will of God.

HOLY SPIRIT GIVES ENABLEMENT

When we receive the baptism in the Holy Spirit, we are to begin to speak! The Holy Spirit will give the vocal inspiration. We cannot speak two languages at one time. We are to speak in our heavenly language. We are not to think in this language since "our understanding is unfruitful" when speaking in tongues. What are we then, to speak?

They Began to Speak

Acts 2:4 And they were all filled with the Holy Spirit and began to speak with other tongues, as the Spirit gave them utterance.

We Begin to Speak

All languages are made up of words that are a combination of sounds. If the Spirit is to give us the enablement or vocal inspiration, like on the Day of Pentecost, we must begin to speak but not in a language we know. We, like those early believers must begin to speak sounds out loud. As we begin to center our thoughts on Jesus, having asked for and received the baptism in the Holy Spirit by faith, we must begin to speak. It will be us speaking, as they did on the Day of Pentecost. The Holy Spirit will then give us the ability.

Rivers of Water

The language that will begin to flow from us will be like "rivers of living water" as it flows from our innermost being.

Even as God made the water hard under Peter's feet when he stepped out of the boat and began walking on the water, the Holy Spirit will make the sounds "hard" under our tongues when we begin to boldly speak out loud.

RECEIVING BAPTISM OF HOLY SPIRIT

Pray This Prayer

> **Dear Heavenly Father,**
>
> I thank You for the gift of salvation!
>
> But Father, I want every gift you have for me. I want your gift of the Holy Spirit! I need His power in my life!
>
> Jesus, I ask you to baptize me in the Holy Spirit! I receive this gift by faith!
>
> Right now, Father, I raise my hands in praise to you. I open my mouth wide and I will begin to praise you, but not in any language I know.
>
> Just like on the day of Pentecost, I'm going to begin to speak. And as I do, I thank you Father, that the Holy spirit is going to give me the ability to do so!

Practical Instructions

Now, with your hands raised in praise to God, begin to praise Him. Begin to speak out loud in little sounds. Rivers of living water will begin to pour from you, as the Holy Spirit gives you the vocal inspiration.

Keep worshiping and praising God out loud in your new heavenly language until you have a free flow of praise to God.

Let Him flow from deep within your spirit.

Let your voice join with the voices of the angels in praise and worship unto God.

PURPOSES OF HEAVENLY LANGUAGE

Praise

> ### *Singing in the Spirit*

When we sing in the spirit, the Holy Spirit not only gives us the sounds, He also give us the melody. Begin to worship God now by singing in your heavenly language.

1 Corinthians 14:15 What is the result then? I will pray with the spirit, and I will also pray with the understanding. I will sing with the spirit, and I will also sing with the understanding.

Our "heavenly" language or "prayer" language is through our spirit up to God. The gift of tongues, with its corresponding gift of interpretation, is God speaking to man.

Prayer

We may not know how to pray about a certain person or situation. When we begin to intercede in tongues, the Holy Spirit is praying through our spirit without the limitations of our minds. We will be praying in perfect harmony with the will of God.

Powerful results can be expected!

As we praise and worship God and intercede on a continuous and daily basis in our new language, great power will continue to flow out of our lives. As we pray and praise "in the spirit," rivers of living water will continue to flow. We will be built up in the faith by praying in the Spirit.

Jude 1:20 But you, beloved, building yourselves up on your most holy faith, praying in the Holy Spirit ...

Sign to Unbelievers

God desires to confirm His Word when we share the gospel by the supernatural manifestation of speaking in tongues. We should never hide or feel that unbelievers would be offended if we speak in tongues. It is a sign given by God to be openly used by believers.

1 Corinthians 14:22a Therefore tongues are for a sign, not to those who believe but to unbelievers ...

> ### *Example at Pentecost*

Acts 2:4,5 And they were all filled with the Holy Spirit and began to speak with other tongues, as the Spirit gave them utterance. Now there were dwelling in Jerusalem Jews, devout men, from every nation under heaven.

The gift of tongues is a sign to the unbeliever, they listen, are amazed and then believe.

➤ *Attracted Multitude*

vs. 6-8 And when this sound occurred, the multitude came together, and were confused, because everyone heard them speak in his own language. Then they were all amazed and marveled, saying to one another, "Look, are not all these who speak Galileans? And how is it that we hear, each in our own language in which we were born?"

➤ *Declaring Wonders of God*

vs. 9-12 "Parthians and Medes and Elamites, those dwelling in Mesopotamia, Judea and Cappadocia, Pontus and Asia, Phrygia and Pamphylia, Egypt and the parts of Libya adjoining Cyrene, visitors from Rome, both Jews and proselytes, Cretans and Arabs--we hear them speaking in our own tongues the wonderful works of God."

So they were all amazed and perplexed, saying to one another, "Whatever could this mean?"

➤ *Supernaturally Speaking in Known Language*

Jesus said that speaking in tongues would be one of the signs which would follow every believer when they "preach" the gospel. As happened on the Day of Pentecost, occasionally unknown to the one speaking in tongues, they're speaking in a language known to someone who's hearing them speak. There are many examples of this happening today. Always it is a supernatural sign to unbelievers that can lead them to receiving the message of the Gospel.

Supernaturally Natural

Speaking in tongues is one of the signs and wonders that Jesus is restoring to His church today. It is for every believer! Today as in the days of the early church, it is the evidence of having received the baptism in the Holy Spirit. It is a supernatural sign to unbelievers.

We don't need to be emotional or try to act "supernatural" when we speak in tongues. We can speak either loudly or softly, rapidly or slowly, when we are led by the Holy Spirit. Let the gift of tongues flow supernaturally and yet in a natural manner.

QUESTIONS FOR REVIEW

1. Explain our part versus God's part in the supernatural manifestation of speaking in tongues.

2. Should speaking in tongues be a one time, or occasional experience in the life of a believer?

3. Should we be concerned about offending unbelievers if they hear us speaking in tongues?

Lesson Four

Important Ministry Tools

Introduction

The gifts of the Holy Spirit provide a whole new way of living for the spirit-filled believer. Even as Peter climbed out of his boat and walked on the water, we are to step out of the comfort zones of natural living and walk on "spiritual waters." We are to live in the spirit and operate in all nine of His supernatural gifts in our daily lives.

1 Samuel 10:6 (NIV) The Spirit of the Lord will come upon you in power, and you will prophesy with them; and you will be changed into a different person.

TOOLS FOR ALL BELIEVERS

Knowledge

It is important that all believers know and understand how to operate in all the gifts of the Holy Spirit. Paul told us this at the very beginning of his teaching on the gifts of the Holy Spirit.

1 Corinthians 12:1 Now concerning spiritual gifts, brethren, I do not want you to be ignorant.

Door to Gifts

The baptism in the Holy Spirit is the entrance into these gifts. We are to begin to operate in the gifts of the Holy Spirit immediately after we receive the baptism in the Holy Spirit. The power of the Holy Spirit has come into us at that moment and we must begin to release that power through one of the manifestations of the Holy Spirit.

Joel 2:28 And it shall come to pass afterward that I will pour out My Spirit on all flesh; your sons and your daughters shall prophesy, your old men shall dream dreams, your young men shall see visions.

Acts 1:8 But you shall receive power when the Holy Spirit has come upon you; and you shall be witnesses to Me in Jerusalem, and in all Judea and Samaria, and to the end of the earth.

Nine Spiritual Gifts

1 Corinthians 12:4-10 Now there are diversities of gifts, but the same Spirit. There are differences of ministries, but the same Lord. And there are diversities of activities, but it is the same God who works all in all.

But the manifestation of the Spirit is given to each one for the profit of all:

For to one is given the word of wisdom through the Spirit, to another the word of knowledge through the same Spirit, to another faith by the same Spirit, to another gifts of healings by the same Spirit, to another the working of miracles, to another prophecy, to another discerning of spirits, to another different kinds of tongues, to another the interpretation of tongues.

Note: The **New International Version** uses the term "distinguishing between spirits." Since this is a much more descriptive title for the gift of the discerning of spirits, we will use it throughout this study.

ALL GIFTS FOR EVERY BELIEVER

In verse seven, the gifts of the Spirit are called the manifestations of the Spirit. They are all given to every believer for the common good. For a believer to fail to operate in any one of the nine gifts of the Holy Spirit would be to miss out on that which is for the "profit of all." That believer would be missing out on the important results of spiritual growth and effective ministry that God has planned for his life.

1 Corinthians 12:7 But the manifestation of the Spirit is given to each one for the profit of all ...

Total Body Ministry

As Paul taught concerning the gifts of the Holy Spirit in 1 Corinthians, he was also addressing the functions of the gifts within the church meeting. In 1 Corinthians 11, he discussed the proper dress in the church and then at the end of that chapter the proper attitude in taking the Lord's Supper.

There has been a lot of confusion concerning the use of the words in verse eight "to one is given" and "to another." From the use of these words, we have been taught that we are each to function in only one gift, or maybe two. This teaching is in error.

Paul was teaching how the gifts are to function in the church meeting. One person isn't to operate in all of the gifts in every meeting. The church meeting is to be a body ministry. One will operate in this gift, another in that.

As we are sensitive to the Holy Spirit, every believer can minister to other members of the body through the gifts of the Holy Spirit. We are all equally important to one another when we allow the gifts of the Holy Spirit to flow.

1 Corinthians 12:11,12 But one and the same Spirit works all these things, distributing to each one individually as He wills. For as the body is one and has many members, but all the members of that one body, being many, are one body, so also is Christ.

Seek Gifts to Build Church

We are to seek spiritual gifts not to lift up ourselves, but that we may be part in edifying the body of Christ.

1 Corinthians 14:12 Even so you, since you are zealous for spiritual gifts, let it be for the edification of the church that you seek to excel.

Notice the use of the word "gifts" is plural.

All the gifts are to edify the whole body of Christ, not just to lift up one person to importance.

Every believer has a ministry. Some believers are called by God into the five-fold ministry (Apostle, Prophet, Teacher, Evangelist or Pastor). The nine spiritual gifts may operate more freely through these believers because they're more prone to allow the Holy Spirit to flow in this manner. As they begin to operate more in one area than another, these gifts may become prominent in their ministry.

Every believer should operate in all of the gifts. They mustn't be afraid of looking foolish. They must be willing to step out and risk making mistakes. That is the only way to learn.

Of all the disciples, only Peter walked on the water. He was the one who was willing to take the risk of stepping out of the boat.

Eagerly Desire Greater Gifts

1 Corinthians 12:31 But earnestly desire the best gifts. And yet I show you a more excellent way.

The greatest gifts for each believer to have fluently operating in their lives are the ones which are needed for each occasion to fulfill the ministry that God has given them.

EXAMPLES OF DILIGENTLY SEEKING GOD

Example of Jacob

Genesis 32:24-30 Then Jacob was left alone; and a Man wrestled with him until the breaking of day. Now when He saw that He did not prevail against him, He touched the socket of his hip; and the socket of Jacob's hip was out of joint as He wrestled with him. And He said, "Let Me go, for the day breaks."

But he said, "I will not let You go unless You bless me!"

So He said to him, "What is your name?"

And he said, "Jacob."

And He said, "Your name shall no longer be called Jacob, but Israel; for you have struggled with God and with men, and have prevailed."

Then Jacob asked Him, saying, "Tell me Your name, I pray."

And He said, "Why is it that you ask about My name?"

And He blessed him there. And Jacob called the name of the place Peniel: "For I have seen God face to face, and my life is preserved."

Jesus Tells Parable

➤ *Asking for Bread*

Luke 11:5-13 And He said to them, "Which of you shall have a friend, and go to him at midnight and say to him, 'Friend, lend me three loaves; for a friend of mine has come to me on his journey, and I have nothing to set before him'; and he will answer from within and say, 'Do not trouble me; the door is now shut, and my children are with me in bed; I cannot rise and give to you'?

"I say to you, though he will not rise and give to him because he is his friend, yet because of his persistence he will rise and give him as many as he needs.

➤ *Ask, Seek, Knock*

"And I say to you, ask, and it will be given to you; seek, and you will find; knock, and it will be opened to you. For everyone who asks receives, and he who seeks finds, and to him who knocks it will be opened. If a son asks for bread from any father among you, will he give him a stone? Or if he asks for a fish, will he give him a serpent instead of a fish? Or if he asks for an egg, will he offer him a scorpion? If you then, being evil, know how to give good gifts to your children, how much more will your heavenly Father give the Holy Spirit to those who ask Him!"

Stir up Gifts

2 Timothy 1:6 Therefore I remind you to stir up the gift of God which is in you through the laying on of my hands.

YIELD YOURSELF TO GOD

Present Yourself

Romans 6:13 And do not present your members as instruments of unrighteousness to sin, but present yourselves to God as being alive from the dead, and your members as instruments of righteousness to God.

Romans 12:1 I beseech you therefore, brethren, by the mercies of God, that you present your bodies a living sacrifice, holy, acceptable to God, which is your reasonable service.

Move into Spirit Realm

As Spirit-filled believers, we are no longer to walk by our old natural means. We must learn to live in a new supernatural dimension, in the realm of the Holy Spirit. As we live by the Spirit, we will continually be sensitive to Him. We will be supernaturally natural. The operation of the spiritual gifts will be a daily part of our lives.

1 Corinthians 2:14 But the natural man does not receive the things of the Spirit of God, for they are foolishness to him; nor can he know them, because they are spiritually discerned.

Galatians 5:25 If we live in the Spirit, let us also walk in the Spirit.

QUESTIONS FOR REVIEW

1. List the nine gifts of the Holy Spirit.

2. Since the gifts of the Holy Spirit are given to every believer to profit all, why do some gifts tend to operate more freely through certain believers?

3. Why should we desire the "greater gifts" which are especially important to the fulfillment of the ministry to which God has called us?

Lesson Five

The Gifts Categorized and Defined

(**Note to the Teacher**: For this lesson you should prepare examples from your own experience to illustrate the operation of the gifts of The Holy Spirit, and then encourage sharing by students as to the operations of these gifts in their lives. This will make the operation and difference of the gifts more clearly understood.)

NINE SCRIPTURES SPEAKING OF THE SPIRITUAL GIFTS

1 Corinthians 12:1 Now concerning spiritual gifts, brethren, I do not want you to be ignorant ...

1 Corinthians 13:2 And though I have the gift of prophecy, and understand all mysteries and all knowledge, and though I have all faith, so that I could remove mountains, but have not love, I am nothing.

1 Corinthians 14:1,12 Pursue love, and desire spiritual gifts, but especially that you may prophesy.

Even so you, since you are zealous for spiritual gifts, let it be for the edification of the church that you seek to excel.

2 Timothy 1:6 Therefore I remind you to stir up the gift of God which is in you through the laying on of my hands.

Hebrews 2:4 God also bearing witness both with signs and wonders, with various miracles, and gifts of the Holy Spirit, according to His own will.

1 Peter 4:10 As each one has received a gift, minister it to one another, as good stewards of the manifold grace of God.

Romans 1:11 For I long to see you, that I may impart to you some spiritual gift, so that you may be established.

Proverbs 18:16 A man's gift makes room for him, and brings him before great men.

NINE GIFTS OF THE SPIRIT

The nine gifts of the Spirit are areas in which the Holy Spirit manifests His Presence. They are expressions of God's grace at work in the world today. They are manifestations of God's power ministering for the good of mankind.

1 Corinthians 12:7-10 But the manifestation of the Spirit is given to each one for the profit of all: for to one is given the word of wisdom through the Spirit, to another the word of knowledge through the same Spirit, to another faith by the same Spirit, to another gifts of healings by the same Spirit, to another the working of miracles, to another prophecy, to another discerning of spirits, to another different kinds of tongues, to another the interpretation of tongues.

Gifts for Everyone

God never intended for people to survive in this world without being part of the spirit realm. Through the baptism in the Holy Spirit, they're given every gift needed to win the battles of this life.

➢ God is Spirit.

➢ Satan is a spirit.

➢ Man is a spirit.

Ephesians 6:12 For we do not wrestle against flesh and blood, but against principalities, against powers, against the rulers of the darkness of this age, against spiritual hosts of wickedness in the heavenly places.

The gifts of the Holy Spirit are given to us to use. They are not "trophies" dispensed for faithful service. The gifts are tools which equip the believer for battle in this life.

THREE GROUPS OR CATEGORIES

Gifts of Vocal Inspiration – (Speaking)

Tongues
Interpretation of Tongues
Prophecy

Revelation Gifts – (Hearing)

Distinguishing Between Spirits
Word of Knowledge
Word of Wisdom

Power Gifts – (Doing)

Gift of Faith
Gifts of Healing
Working of Miracles

GIFTS OF VOCAL INSPIRATION

The first three gifts we will study are the utterance gifts or gifts of vocal inspiration. They are the Holy Spirit speaking to us, and through us.

The gifts of vocal inspiration are manifested when God speaks supernaturally to believers. As believers operate in these gifts others are strengthened, encouraged and comforted. While God will bring correction He will never bring condemnation through these gifts.

Tongues

The gift of tongues is a supernatural vocal expression of an inspiration given by the Holy Spirit using the normal voice organs.

It is a language never learned by the speaker, nor understood by the mind of the speaker.

The spoken language may be a heavenly language used by the angels, or a human language.

The gift of tongues may possibly be understood by the hearer in their own language.

Interpretation

The gift of interpretation of tongues is the supernatural showing forth by the Spirit of the explanation or meaning of a vocal expression of a message in another tongue.

It isn't an operation, or understanding, of the mind. It is given by the Spirit of God.

Interpretation means to explain, expound, or unfold. It isn't a literal, word for word, translation.

Prophecy

The gift of prophecy is a spontaneous, supernatural vocal expression of inspiration in a known tongue which strengthens, encourages, and comforts the body of Christ.

It is a direct message from God to a particular person, or group of people.

REVELATION GIFTS

The gifts of revelation are God revealing spirits, knowledge, or wisdom to His people for particular situations. These gifts can be given to us through tongues and interpretation or the gift of prophecy. They can be given to us through dreams, visions, or an inner knowing.

Distinguishing Between Spirits

The distinguishing between spirits is a supernatural insight into the spirit world. It shows the category of spirit, or spirits, behind a person, a situation, an action or a message.

Three areas of spirits to be distinguished are:

➤ **Of God** – God and His angels
➤ **From Satan** – Satan and his demons
➤ **The human spirit** – the flesh, or natural man

Word of Knowledge

The word of knowledge is the supernatural revelation by the Holy Spirit of certain facts, present or past, about a person or situation, which were not learned through the natural mind. This gift gives information from God which couldn't be known naturally.

This gift is a word, a part, not the whole picture, not all God's knowledge on any subject. It deals with actual information. It shows us the way things are now.

Word of Wisdom

The word of wisdom is a supernatural revelation by the Holy Spirit giving the believer God's wisdom on how to proceed on a course of action based on natural, or supernatural, knowledge. It reveals God's plan and purpose for our life and ministry. It reveals what God would like done immediately, in a short while, or in the near or distant future. It reveals what an individual or corporate gathering should do and how to proceed in God's will. The word of wisdom often operates with the word of knowledge.

POWER GIFTS

The power gifts are God releasing His power to flow through us. They are God doing something through us!

➤ God speaks to us – vocal gifts.
➤ He reveals things to us – revelation gifts.
➤ He releases through us His power to act – power gifts.

Gift of Faith

The gift of faith is a supernatural faith for a specific time and purpose. It is a gift of power to accomplish a certain task in whatever situation you are in at that particular time.

Working of Miracles

The working of miracles is a supernatural intervention in the ordinary course of nature. It is the demonstration of the power of God by which the laws of nature are altered, suspended or controlled for a time.

The working of miracles is a temporary interruption and suspension of the natural and accustomed order by a manifestation of God's supernatural power.

Gifts of Healings

The gifts of healings are the supernatural impartations of God's healing power into people. They are described as gifts (plural) since there are many ways to impart, or minister healing to the sick.

They are supernatural manifestations of the Holy Spirit and are not the same as medical science.

SEEK THE GIFT-GIVER AND THE GIFTS

Hunger and Thirst

Matthew 5:6 Blessed are those who hunger and thirst for righteousness, for they shall be filled.

Seek Mind of Spirit

Romans 8:5,6 For those who live according to the flesh set their minds on the things of the flesh, but those who live according to the Spirit, the things of the Spirit.

For to be carnally minded is death, but to be spiritually minded is life and peace.

Romans 8:13,14 For if you live according to the flesh you will die; but if by the Spirit you put to death the deeds of the body, you will live. For as many as are led by the Spirit of God, these are sons of God.

Receive Manifestation

1 Corinthians 12:7 But the manifestation of the Spirit is given to each one for the profit of all.

John 14:12 Most assuredly, I say to you, he who believes in Me, the works that I do he will do also; and greater works than these he will do, because I go to My Father.

2 Timothy 1:6 Therefore I remind you to stir up the gift of God which is in you through the laying on of my hands.

Continually, keep all the gifts of the Spirit fanned into flame within yourself!

QUESTIONS FOR REVIEW

1. List and define each of the vocal inspiration gifts.
2. List and define each of the revelation gifts.
3. List and define each of the power gifts.

Lesson Six

Vocal Inspiration Gifts
Tongues and Interpretation

1 Corinthians 12:8-10 For to one is given the word of wisdom through the Spirit, to another the word of knowledge through the same Spirit, to another faith by the same Spirit, to another gifts of healings by the same Spirit, to another the working of miracles, to another prophecy, to another discerning of spirits, to another different kinds of tongues, to another the interpretation of tongues.

Nine Gifts of the Holy Spirit		
Vocal Inspiration	**Revelation**	**Power**
✥ **Tongues**	Distinguishing between Spirits	Gift of Faith
✥ **Interpretation of Tongues**	Word of Knowledge	Gifts of Healings
Prophecy	Word of Wisdom	Working of Miracles

GIFTS OF TONGUES – INTERPRETATION – PROPHECY

Introduction

The gifts of vocal inspiration are manifested when God speaks supernaturally to believers. When believers operate in these gifts, others are strengthened, encouraged and comforted. While God may bring correction, He will never bring condemnation through these gifts.

1 Corinthians 14:3 But he who prophesies speaks edification and exhortation and comfort to men.

Realizing that these gifts are subject to the fallibility of the human vessel who is speaking, the word that is delivered is never to be considered with the same authority as Scripture. It must always be judged and weighed carefully as to whether it is from God.

1 Corinthians 14:29 Let two or three prophets speak, and let the others judge.

For All Believers

As we studied in Lesson Three, the manifestation of tongues is for all believers when they receive the baptism in the Holy Spirit. Paul instructed believers to pray that they would be given the interpretation.

1 Corinthians 14:13 Therefore let him who speaks in a tongue pray that he may interpret.

Paul also states that the gift of prophecy is of more benefit than the gift of tongues and that his desire was that all prophesy.

1 Corinthians 14:5 I wish you all spoke with tongues, but even more that you prophesied; for he who prophesies is greater than he who speaks with tongues, unless indeed he interprets, that the church may receive edification.

All are to speak in tongues. All are to pray that they may interpret, yet it is better to prophesy. From these teachings of Paul we can assume that all three gifts of vocal inspiration are for every believer.

VOCAL INSPIRATION GIFTS COMPARED

Tongues and Interpretation

The gifts of tongues and interpretation of tongues are the easiest gifts to exercise. They are the most common, and therefore, the most abused.

A message must be given in tongues before someone else can receive the message from God through the gift of interpretation. So, the gifts of tongues and interpretation flow together.

Tongues and Prophecy

When one speaks in their supernatural language, he is speaking mysteries to God.

1 Corinthians 14:2-5,39 For he who speaks in a tongue does not speak to men but to God, for no one understands him; however, in the spirit he speaks mysteries.

When one gives a prophecy he is helping other believers.

v.3 But he who prophesies speaks edification and exhortation and comfort to men.

Speaking in tongues builds up, or edifies, the individual believer in the Spirit. The gift of prophecy builds up the church.

v. 4 He who speaks in a tongue edifies himself, but he who prophesies edifies the church.

Prophecy is greater because it directly edifies the church.

v.5 I wish you all spoke with tongues, but even more that you prophesied; for he who prophesies is greater than he who speaks with tongues, unless indeed he interprets, that the church may receive edification.

The word "church" is used nine times in this chapter indicating the importance of the use of the gifts for the church.

Why Tongues?
Why Prophecy?

Why does God speak through tongues and interpretation at one time and through the gift of prophecy at another?

1 Corinthians 14:22 Therefore tongues are for a sign, not to those who believe but to unbelievers; but prophesying is not for unbelievers but for those who believe.

Tongues are for a sign to the unbeliever. The interpretation of tongues is God's message to His body.

Prophecy is for the believer. Prophecy requires a higher level of faith to operate when no tongues are given first to release the manifestation of this gift.

GIFT OF TONGUES

Definition

The gift of tongues is a supernatural vocal expression of inspiration given by the Holy Spirit using the normal voice. It is a language never learned by the speaker, nor understood by the mind of the speaker.

The spoken message may be a heavenly language used by the angels, or a human language. The gift of tongues may possibly be understood by the listener.

Understanding Tongues

The gift of tongues, one of the nine spiritual gifts, must be distinguished from the manifestation of speaking in tongues which is the supernatural language of praise and intercession which is received when a believer is baptized in the Holy Spirit.

In the gift of tongues, God is speaking to man. The manifestation of our prayer and praise language is the Holy Spirit through man's spirit speaking to God. One is from God to man and the other is from man to God.

Tongues in Operation

When the anointing is on a person and they give in a public meeting, a message in tongues which is not understood by the people, it is to be followed by the gift of interpretation of tongues.

1 Corinthians 14:27 If anyone speaks in a tongue, let there be two or at the most three, each in turn, and let one interpret.

When the entire group is singing in tongues, it is a time of praise which is given directly to the Father. There is no interpretation needed following a time of praise. If there are people in the group which may not understand what has just happened, there should be an explanation of what singing in tongues is.

In Public

A message may be given which is not understood by the person giving the message, but is understood by a person, or persons, standing within hearing range.

Acts 2:4-6 All of them were filled with the Holy Spirit and began to speak in other tongues as the Spirit enabled them.

Now there were staying in Jerusalem God-fearing Jews from every nation under heaven. When they heard this sound, a crowd came together in bewilderment, because each one heard them speaking in his own language.

Purpose

God desires to speak to His people. One way that He does this today is through the operation of the gift of tongues together with the interpretation of tongues.

INSTRUCTIONS FOR USE

Have Anointing

When God desires to give a message to the body in tongues, the person through whom He desires to give that message will sense the prompting of the Holy Spirit to do so. That person will experience an anointing and an urging of the Spirit with the thought from deep within his spirit to give a message in tongues at the next appropriate time in the meeting. He should not interrupt the flow of the meeting, what is presently being done or said, but should wait until the correct time. Remember, the Holy Spirit would never interrupt Himself.

Be Recognized

In larger assemblies of believers, it is best to be recognized by the leadership before giving the message. The Bible says to "know those that labor among you." A message is not to be given unless someone is there who will interpret. Otherwise the one giving the message in tongues will be expected to interpret.

Speak Clearly

The utterance should not be shouted, but spoken clearly with whatever emotion the Spirit is giving. For example, sometimes the Spirit will give the message with boldness, or joy. Express the emotions you feel as you speak.

Have Interpretation

When a message is given, there must be a time of silence while the believers wait for God to give the interpretation though the gift of interpretation.

1 Corinthians 14:19,28 Yet in the church I would rather speak five words with my understanding, that I may teach others also, than ten thousand words in a tongue.

But if there is no interpreter, let him keep silent in church, and let him speak to himself and to God.

Only Three!

Paul instructed the church that there should not be more than three individual messages in tongues in a meeting under normal circumstances.

1 Corinthians 14:27 If anyone speaks in a tongue, let there be two or at the most three, each in turn, and let one interpret.

Not to be Forbidden

Speaking in tongues is the only gift we are commanded not to forbid.

1 Corinthians 14:39 Therefore, brethren, desire earnestly to prophesy, and do not forbid to speak with tongues.

Other Gifts

When the gift of tongues is in operation, the gift of interpretation and the gift of distinguishing between spirits are also in operation. This will be discussed more in the teaching on these gifts.

GIFT OF INTERPRETATION

Definition

The gift of interpretation of tongues is the supernatural showing forth by the Spirit of the explanation, or meaning, in the hearers own language, of a vocal expression of a message in another tongue.

It is not an operation, or understanding, of the mind. It is given by the Spirit of God.

Interpretation means to explain, expound, or unfold. It is not a literal, word for word, translation.

A person speaking in a foreign country may need an interpreter. This is not a gift of the Spirit, but rather a person who understands and speaks both languages fluently.

Not Same Length

The interpretation may not be the same length as the original message in tongues for two reasons.

This is not an actual translation. It is an interpretation and may not take as many words to state what has been said in the Spirit, or it may take more words.

The person giving the interpretation may move on into the gift of prophecy. There is usually a different anointing and after you are aware of the moving of the Holy Spirit you will know the difference.

Purpose

The gift of interpretation has one main purpose which is to make the gift of tongues intelligible to the hearers so that the church may know what has been said and can be edified.

OPERATION OF GIFT OF INTERPRETATION

In Public

The same rules apply for the operation of the gift of interpretation which apply to speaking in tongues in a public meeting. The Holy Spirit will never do anything in confusion or in a disruptive manner.

One person may speak the message in tongues and then give the interpretation himself.

One person may speak and another person give the interpretation.

Sometimes one person may start an interpretation and another person take it up and finish it. This may happen when a person is new in operating in interpretation and becomes frightened when he is stepping out in faith. Then a more experienced person in the gift of interpretation of tongues may finish the message. A competitive spirit must never be allowed in the operation of the gifts of the Spirit. An attitude of "I can give a better rendition than that" is not of God.

In the operation of the gifts of the Spirit, it is always necessary that the gift of distinguishing between spirits be in operation. When the gifts are operating freely in a meeting, the person in charge is responsible to discern the spirits of each operation and to stop anything which is contrary to the Word and/or the Spirit of God.

In Private

Paul stated that he prayed in tongues more than others, but he went on to say that in a service he spoke in prophecy. If he did not speak in tongues in the service, he must have been writing about speaking in tongues in private.

Paul also instructs us to pray for the gift of interpretation.

1 Corinthians 14:13-15 Therefore let him who speaks in a tongue pray that he may interpret. For if I pray in a tongue, my spirit prays, but my understanding is unfruitful. What is the result then? I will pray with the spirit, and I will also pray with the understanding. I will sing with the spirit, and I will also sing with the understanding.

As we pray in tongues in private, we may be led to ask God to give us the interpretation. Often when we are troubled about a situation and begin to pray in tongues, we will then begin to pray in our own language. We may find ourselves praying things we do not even know, or asking God to handle the problem in a way that we have not understood before. That is the gift of interpretation of tongues operating in our private prayer life.

It is not necessary that we interpret everything we privately pray in tongues. Many times we are praising God and it needs no interpretation. Or, perhaps in the Spirit we have been praying the answer but God does not want the answer revealed to us at that time.

1 Corinthians 14:2 For he who speaks in a tongue does not speak to men but to God, for no one understands him; however, in the spirit he speaks mysteries.

As we operate in the gift of interpretation in private, we are preparing ourselves to operate in the gift of interpretation in public.

RECEIVING THIS GIFT

With all the gifts of the Spirit, a person must be in a proper relationship with God for the gift to operate freely.

We are instructed to ask the Father for a free operation of the gifts most needed in our ministry, so the first step is to ask! When the interpretation comes it may be with a few beginning words, and the rest will come when we speak those words out in faith. We may receive pictures, symbols, or a thought. Sometimes a message is given in song, and the interpretation may be given in song also.

Warning!

A person will never be given an interpretation of tongues which is condemning because condemnation comes from Satan.

A person will never be given an interpretation which contradicts the Word of God.

A continued interpretation will never correct what another person operating in the gift of interpretation of tongues has said. The leader, in love, may be required to correct a person who is not flowing in the Spirit and then ask for, or give the proper interpretation.

The Holy Spirit has also given us the gift of distinguishing between spirits and it is very important that this gift be in operation when the gifts of vocal inspiration are being exercised. We will study this more in the lesson on distinguishing between spirits. However, for now it is important to understand that just as we are to pray for the gift of interpretation when a message is given in tongues we are to pray for the gift of distinguishing between spirits. God never makes a mistake, but we are all human, and humans do make mistakes. God has given each of us the responsibility of knowing which spirit we are hearing.

JESUS AND VOCAL INSPIRATION GIFTS

Jesus operated in all of the gifts of the Spirit except the gifts of tongues and interpretation. We have no recorded instance of these two gifts being used in His life.

Exercise

It is important that we not spend our time just learning the facts. Tongues and interpretation can only be understood when they are allowed to operate!

As you have come to the end of this lesson enter into a time of praise and allow the Holy Spirit to operate though you in the gifts of tongues and interpretation.

QUESTIONS FOR REVIEW

1. Explain in your own words what the gift of tongues is.

2. Explain what the gift of interpretation of tongues is.

3. How should a message in tongues or interpretation of tongues be given?

Lesson Seven

Vocal Inspiration Gift
Gift of Prophecy

1 Corinthians 12:8-10 To one there is given through the Spirit the message of wisdom, to another the message of knowledge by means of the same Spirit, to another faith by the same Spirit, to another gifts of healing by that one Spirit, to another miraculous powers, to another prophecy, to another distinguishing between spirits, to another speaking in different kinds of tongues, and to still another the interpretation of tongues.

Nine Gifts of the Holy Spirit		
Vocal Inspiration	**Revelation**	**Power**
Tongues	Distinguishing between Spirits	Gift of Faith
Interpretation of Tongues	Word of Knowledge	Gifts of Healings
✣ **Prophecy**	Word of Wisdom	Working of Miracles

GIFT OF PROPHECY

Definition

The gift of prophecy is a spontaneous, supernatural vocal expression of inspiration in a known tongue which strengthens, encourages, and comforts the body of Christ. It is a direct message from God to a particular person or group of people.

The Greek word for prophecy is "propheteia" meaning speaking the mind and counsel of God.

Purpose

The purpose of the gift of prophecy is for strengthening, encouragement, and comfort.

1 Corinthians 14:3 But everyone who prophesies speaks to men for their strengthening, encouragement and comfort.

➢ *Strengthens or Edifies*

In its root meaning, "strengthens" or "edifies" signifies to erect, or build up.

1 Corinthians 14:4,5 He who speaks in a tongue edifies himself, but he who prophesies edifies the church. I would like every one of you to speak in tongues, but I would rather have you prophesy. He who prophesies is greater than one who speaks in tongues, unless he interprets, so that the church may be edified.

➤ *Encourage or Exhort*

The word translated "encourage" is a Greek word meaning a calling nearer to God. The dictionary says "encourage" is to give courage, to inspire with hope, or to give boldness.

➤ *Comfort*

Going back to 1 Corinthians 14:3 the Greek word, "paramuthia," means primarily a speaking closely to anyone, and denotes consolation. The dictionary says "comfort" is to lighten or lessen grief or trouble, to console, cheer or gladden.

PROPHECY IS

Part of Mind of God

Prophecy is part of the mind of God – not the total picture.

1 Corinthians 13:9 For we know in part and we prophesy in part.

Greatest Gift of Three

Prophecy is the greatest of the gifts of vocal inspiration.

1 Corinthians 14:1,5,39 Pursue love, and desire spiritual gifts, but especially that you may prophesy.

I wish you all spoke with tongues, but even more that you prophesied; for he who prophesies is greater than he who speaks with tongues, unless indeed he interprets, that the church may receive edification.

Therefore, brethren, desire earnestly to prophesy, and do not forbid to speak with tongues.

Sign to Unbelievers

1 Corinthians 14:24,25 But if all prophesy, and an unbeliever or an uninformed person comes in, he is convinced by all, he is judged by all. And thus the secrets of his heart are revealed; and so, falling down on his face, he will worship God and report that God is truly among you.

Not Irrevocable

Jeremiah 18:7,8 The instant I speak concerning a nation and concerning a kingdom, to pluck up, to pull down, and to destroy it, if that nation against whom I have spoken turns from its evil, I will relent of the disaster that I thought to bring upon it.

GIFTS TO BE JUDGED

Warnings!

Prophecy is for a particular group of people, at a particular time, through a particular person. It should not be given the same credence which is given to the written Word of God.

The person, or persons, hearing the prophecy may give the message a different connotation than what the Spirit of God said.

The person giving the prophecy is human, and therefore fallible. Some so-called "prophecies" are given out of wishful thinking, special interest or concerns of the deliverer, or even from a lying spirit.

The person giving a prophecy in a body of believers should be known to that body of believers. If the person is a stranger to the group but feels he has a prophecy, he should identify himself and ask permission of the leader of the group before he speaks.

Weigh Carefully

Prophecy, tongues, and the interpretation of tongues are to be judged by the Word and by the Spirit.

The gifts of vocal inspiration are to be weighed carefully by the person, or persons, hearing the message.

1 Corinthians 14:29-32 Let two or three prophets speak, and let the others judge. But if anything is revealed to another who sits by, let the first keep silent. For you can all prophesy one by one, that all may learn and all may be encouraged. And the spirits of the prophets are subject to the prophets.

Judge

Paul, though an apostle, instructed them to judge his message.

1 Corinthians 10:15 I speak as to wise men; judge for yourselves what I say.

SEVEN TESTS TO GIVE PROPHECY, TONGUES, INTERPRETATION

Agrees with Scripture

A spoken "word" from God would never contradict His written Word. God does not change His teaching. We are to judge anything which seems new by all the teachings on that subject in the scripture. There cannot be a conflict.

Galatians 1:8 But even if we, or an angel from heaven, preach any other gospel to you than what we have preached to you, let him be accursed.

Fruit in Person's Life

It is true that only God can judge a person, but everyone of us is responsible to know the fruits of those we receive "truths" from.

Matthew 7:15,16a Beware of false prophets, who come to you in sheep's clothing, but inwardly they are ravenous wolves. You will know them by their fruits.

Glorifies Christ

Does the message glorify Christ? Does the message bring glory to the person to whom the message is given?

John 16:13,14 However, when He, the Spirit of truth, has come, He will guide you into all truth; for He will not speak on His own authority, but whatever He hears He will speak; and He will tell you things to come. He will glorify Me, for He will take of what is Mine and declare it to you.

Revelation 19:10b For the testimony of Jesus is the spirit of prophecy.

Is Fulfilled

If a message is from God, it will come to pass. Perhaps, not in our time frame, but it will happen.

Deuteronomy 18:20-22 But the prophet who presumes to speak a word in My name, which I have not commanded him to speak, or who speaks in the name of other gods, that prophet shall die.

And if you say in your heart, 'How shall we know the word which the LORD has not spoken?'– when a prophet speaks in the name of the LORD, if the thing does not happen or come to pass, that is the thing which the LORD has not spoken; the prophet has spoken it presumptuously; you shall not be afraid of him."

Ezekiel 12:25 "For I am the LORD. I speak, and the word which I speak will come to pass; it will no more be postponed; for in your days, O rebellious house, I will say the word and perform it," says the Lord God.

Leads Toward God

There are false prophecies and there are false prophets. A prophecy from the Lord will always lead us closer to Him. A message from Satan will lead us away from God!

Deuteronomy 13:1-3 If there arises among you a prophet or a dreamer of dreams, and he gives you a sign or a wonder, and the sign or the wonder of which he spoke to you comes to pass, saying, 'Let us go after other gods which you have not known,

and let us serve them,' you shall not listen to the words of that prophet or that dreamer of dreams, for the LORD your God is testing you to know whether you love the LORD your God with all your heart and with all your soul.

Brings Liberty

If the message causes a person who is seeking to serve God to feel depressed, grieved, or heavy in their spirit, it is not from God.

1 Corinthians 14:3 But he who prophesies speaks edification and exhortation and comfort to men.

Romans 8:15 For you did not receive the spirit of bondage again to fear, but you received the Spirit of adoption by whom we cry out, "Abba, Father."

Inner Witness

We have the Holy Spirit within us and if we will learn to listen, He will witness to us if the message is from God.

1 John 2:20,27 But you have an anointing from the Holy One, and you know all things.

But the anointing which you have received from Him abides in you, and you do not need that anyone teach you; but as the same anointing teaches you concerning all things, and is true, and is not a lie, and just as it has taught you, you will abide in Him.

Ephesians 1:17-19 That the God of our Lord Jesus Christ, the Father of glory, may give to you the spirit of wisdom and revelation in the knowledge of Him, the eyes of your understanding being enlightened; that you may know what is the hope of His calling, what are the riches of the glory of His inheritance in the saints, and what is the exceeding greatness of His power toward us who believe, according to the working of His mighty power ...

PERSONAL PROPHECIES

If a person receives a "personal prophecy," they should judge them by the same seven tests. Only after these tests have been applied should the message be received into their spirits as a true word from the Lord.

Seven Tests

➤ Does it agree with scripture?
➤ What are the fruits in the deliverer's life?
➤ Does it glorify Christ?
➤ Does it lead toward, or away from God?
➤ Does it bring liberty, or bondage?
➤ What is the inner witness of the Spirit?
➤ Is it fulfilled?

Self-Serving

Especially in the area of personal prophecy, one must be aware of "self serving" prophecies. In other words, does the prophecy appeal to the pride of the receiver.

"You are my special one ..."

"I have called you to do something that no one else has ever done ..."

Does it raise the deliverer to a special place of importance?

"Listen to this man/woman for I have sent him to ..."

Confirmation

Does the message confirm what the Lord has already been speaking to you?

If the message is something completely new, but you have tested the spirits and know the person to be of God, keep that message in your spirit and wait for confirmation to come in another way, or through another person.

Judge Them

Personal prophecy has been misused in the past, but that doesn't mean personal prophecies should be thrown out. Instead, take the time necessary to judge them and then receive them. *Judge then receive Not vica versa*

If a prophecy is a warning about a situation or a person that you are involved with or thinking of being involved with, take time to pray the relationship through and ask the Lord for more knowledge in that area.

It is a good practice to write prophecies down so that you can review them in the future. They can be a great source of encouragement and consolation, however again, they must never take the place of God's Word.

GIFT OF PROPHECY COMPARED TO CALLING OF A PROPHET

The gift of prophecy is not the same as a calling to the office of a prophet. God has appointed a five-fold ministry.

Ephesians 4:11 And He Himself gave some to be apostles, some prophets, some evangelists, and some pastors and teachers ...

Ministry Gifting of Prophet

Every believer has the privilege of operating in the gift of prophecy, but not every believer has the calling of a prophet.

1 Corinthians 12:7,28,29 But the manifestation of the Spirit is given to each one for the profit of all.

And God has appointed these in the church: first apostles, second prophets, third teachers, after that miracles, then gifts of healings, helps, administrations, varieties of tongues.

Are all apostles? Are all prophets? Are all teachers? Are all workers of miracles?

For example, the four daughters of Philip operated in the gift of prophecy, but God sent Agabus to Paul as a prophet to deliver a directive prophecy to Paul.

All May Prophesy

1 Corinthians 14:31 For you can all prophesy one by one, that all may learn and all may be encouraged.

Even though the gift of prophecy functions through a person this does not mean they are a prophet.

IS THE GIFT OF PROPHECY FOR TODAY?

The Word of God prophesied that there would be prophecy in our days.

Joel Wrote

Joel 2:28 And it shall come to pass afterward that I will pour out My Spirit on all flesh; your sons and your daughters shall prophesy, your old men shall dream dreams, your young men shall see visions ...

Peter Said

2 Peter 1:19 We also have the prophetic word made more sure, which you do well to heed as a light that shines in a dark place, until the day dawns and the morning star rises in your hearts ...

Luke Quoted

Acts 2:16-18 But this is what was spoken by the prophet Joel: 'And it shall come to pass in the last days, says God, That I will pour out of My Spirit on all flesh; your sons and your daughters shall prophesy, your young men shall see visions, your old men shall dream dreams. And on My menservants and on My maidservants I will pour out My Spirit in those days; and they shall prophesy.'

Paul Explained

1 Corinthians 13:8-13 Love never fails. But whether there are prophecies, they will fail; whether there are tongues, they will cease; whether there is knowledge, it will vanish away. For we know in part and we prophesy in part. But when that which is perfect has come, then that which is in part will be done away. When I was a child, I spoke as a child, I understood as a child, I thought as a child; but when I became a man, I put away childish things.

For now we see in a mirror, dimly, but then face to face. Now I know in part, but then I shall know just as I also am known. And now abide faith, hope, love, these three; but the greatest of these is love.

Until the Perfect Comes

Prophecy will be in the church until "that which is perfect has come."

Some have suggested that the words "when that which is perfect has come" refers to the completed canon of scripture, thereby implying that certain gifts were temporary until the scriptures were completed. However, in context, we see that these words are clearly a reference to the day when we will be face to face with Jesus Christ.

INSTRUCTIONS FOR USE

The gift of prophecy is different from the gift of tongues in that it does not operate at our will. We may receive a prophecy in a private place, or in a meeting.

The gift of prophecy often operates during a time of praise and worship, or following a time of the operation of the gift of tongues and interpretation of tongues.

In Private

We may receive a prophecy about something we have been meditating on or praying about for our own edification. It may, or may not be something which we will share later at a public time.

In Public

➢ *Person in Control*

The person giving the prophecy must be in full control of himself.

1 Corinthians 14:32 And the spirits of the prophets are subject to the prophets.

➢ *Natural Voice*

The prophecy should be given in a natural voice unless the tone of voice is changed by the Holy Spirit for emphasis.

➢ *Contemporary Language*

The prophecy should normally be given in simple, modern and easily understood words. Avoid archaic King

James English which could distract from the simplicity of the message.

> ### Not with Extreme Emotions

A prophecy should not be given with great emotion because that often detracts from the message. It should not be screamed forth, but given in a clear voice.

> ### Refrain from Nervous Repetition

The person giving the prophecy should refrain from repeating the same phrase over and over. "Thus saith the Lord" is often repeated in nervousness. If the message is truly from the Lord, His Spirit will confirm it within the spirits of the listeners.

QUESTIONS FOR REVIEW

1. What is the gift of prophecy?

2. Compare the gift of prophecy to tongues and interpretation.

3. What are seven tests we should use to judge whether any message is from God?

Revelation Gift

Distinguishing Between Spirits

1 Corinthians 12:8-10 For to one is given the word of wisdom through the Spirit, to another the word of knowledge through the same Spirit, to another faith by the same Spirit, to another gifts of healings by the same Spirit, to another the working of miracles, to another prophecy, to another discerning of spirits, to another different kinds of tongues, to another the interpretation of tongues.

Nine Gifts of the Spirit		
Vocal Inspiration	**Revelation**	**Power**
Tongues	♫ **Distinguishing Between Spirits**	Gift of Faith
Interpretation of Tongues	Word of Knowledge	Gifts of Healing
Prophecy	Word of Wisdom	Working of Miracles

THE REVELATION GIFTS

Introduction

The revelation gifts are manifested as God supernaturally reveals the identity, nature or activity of spirits, or when He supernaturally reveals knowledge or wisdom to His people. This revelation comes into our minds through our spirits in the form of a thought, impression, feeling, dream or vision. The three revelation gifts are the discerning of spirits (or distinguishing between spirits), the word of knowledge, and the word of wisdom.

Just as the gifts of vocal inspiration work together, the revelation gifts flow together almost as one. We separate them in this study for the purpose of understanding them. As we learn the various manifestations of the Holy Spirit, we become more free to receive them into our lives.

There may be some confusion in our minds as to whether we are operating in the word of wisdom, word of knowledge, or distinguishing between spirits. One reason for the confusion is that we are often operating in more than one of these gifts. It isn't necessary to know which gift we are receiving. We can simply allow them to flow through us as God wills.

For Example

The gift of distinguishing between spirits may alert us to the fact that the person who has come for prayer has a demonic spirit.

Then a word of wisdom may tell us when and how to minister to the person for immediate results.

DISTINGUISHING BETWEEN SPIRITS

Definition

The gift of distinguishing between spirits is a supernatural insight into the realm of the spirit world. It reveals the type of spirit, or spirits, behind a person, a situation, an action or a message. It is a knowing in your spirit which comes by supernatural revelation concerning the source, nature, and activity of any spirit.

The word "distinguishing" in Greek is "diakrisis" and it means a clear discrimination.

It's Not

It isn't the "gift of discernment" – there is no such gift mentioned in the Bible. The New King James Version refers to the gift of discerning of spirits, not the gift of discernment. Discernment is an operation of human wisdom in the area of the soul.

Distinguishing between spirits isn't mind reading, or mental penetration, or psychological insight. It isn't being critical or judging.

The distinguishing between spirits isn't discerning of character, or faults.

Matthew 7:1 Judge not, that you be not judged.

THREE AREAS OF SPIRIT ACTIVITY

When we are operating in the distinguishing between spirits, it's important that we understand there are three areas of spirit activity. Distinguishing between spirits will operate in all three of these areas, not just with evil spirits. They are:

➢ Spirit of God

➢ Human Spirit

➢ Satan's Kingdom

Spirit of God

The Spirit of God includes His heavenly angels which are sent to do battle for us and to bring us messages.

Human Spirit

The human spirit makes choices between the Spirit of God and Satan's kingdom or between good and evil. Through the process of life's associations and decisions, the human spirit will reflect either Godly or carnal natures.

The human spirit can be full of the love of God and therefore exhibit pure, loving behavior through the person, or it can be full of hypocrisy, lies and anger, and exhibit hostile, inhuman and selfish behavior.

Satan and Demons

There is the evil kingdom of Satan and his demons. Some examples are spirits of lust, jealousy, pride, lying, witchcraft and rebellion.

PURPOSE OF GIFT OF DISTINGUISHING BETWEEN SPIRITS

When we operate in the gift of distinguishing between spirits, we can test the spirits behind an expression of tongues, interpretation, or prophecy. In deliverance and healing we can know the spirits which are involved.

We don't discern evil spirits only, but also the human spirit of a person, or the presence of angelic beings. At times of need, the believer may be given a strong impression of angels or of evil beings.

With the distinguishing between spirits in operation within the body of Christ:

➤ bound saints can be delivered;

➤ the plans of Satan can be discerned;

➤ sin can be kept out of the midst of the saints;

➤ and false revelation can be detected.

Importance of Gift

All the gifts are for a specific purpose and will profit all. However there has been little taught on the distinguishing between spirits for many years.

1 John 4:1-3 Beloved, do not believe every spirit, but test the spirits, whether they are of God; because many false prophets have gone out into the world. By this you know the Spirit of God: every spirit that confesses that Jesus Christ has come in the flesh is of God, and every spirit that does not confess that Jesus Christ has come in the flesh is not of God. And this is the spirit of the Antichrist, which you have heard was coming, and is now already in the world.

For our Protection

This lack of teaching has left the body of Christ unprotected!

Every believer should pray for the stirring up of the gift of distinguishing between spirits for his own protection, the protection of his family, and the protection of the body of Christ.

DECEPTION

Warning by Apostle Paul

Paul warned of the deception that is all around us.

➤ *False Apostles*
➤ *Deceitful Workers*

2 Corinthians 11:13-15 For such are false apostles, deceitful workers, transforming themselves into apostles of Christ. And no wonder! For Satan himself transforms himself into an angel of light. Therefore it is no great thing if his ministers also transform themselves into ministers of righteousness, whose end will be according to their works.

➤ *Departed from Faith*

1 Timothy 4:1,2 Now the Spirit expressly says that in latter times some will depart from the faith, giving heed to deceiving spirits and doctrines of demons, speaking lies in hypocrisy, having their own conscience seared with a hot iron.

➤ *Having Form of Godliness*

2 Timothy 3:1-9 But know this, that in the last days perilous times will come: for men will be lovers of themselves, lovers of money, boasters, proud, blasphemers, disobedient to parents, unthankful, unholy, unloving, unforgiving, slanderers, without self-control, brutal, despisers of good, traitors, headstrong, haughty, lovers of pleasure rather than lovers of God, having a form of godliness but denying its power.

And from such people turn away! For of this sort are those who creep into households and make captives of gullible women loaded down with sins, led away by various lusts, always learning and never able to come to the knowledge of the truth.

Now as Jannes and Jambres resisted Moses, so do these also resist the truth: men of corrupt minds, disapproved concerning the faith; but they will progress no further, for their folly will be manifest to all, as theirs also was.

➤ *Grow Worse and Worse*

2 Timothy 3:13 But evil men and impostors will grow worse and worse, deceiving and being deceived.

OUR RESPONSIBILITY!

> ### *Test the Spirits*

God didn't intend that we should be defenseless against evil spirits. He has commanded us to test the spirits and He has given us instructions on how this is to be done. He has even given us the gift of distinguishing between spirits so that we may know what's happening around us.

1 John 4:1-6 Beloved, do not believe every spirit, but test the spirits, whether they are of God; because many false prophets have gone out into the world. By this you know the Spirit of God: every spirit that confesses that Jesus Christ has come in the flesh is of God,

> ### *What Is the Test?*

And every spirit that does not confess that Jesus Christ has come in the flesh is not of God. And this is the spirit of the Antichrist, which you have heard was coming, and is now already in the world.

You are of God, little children, and have overcome them, because He who is in you is greater than he who is in the world. They are of the world. Therefore they speak as of the world, and the world hears them. We are of God. He who knows God hears us; he who is not of God does not hear us. By this we know the spirit of truth and the spirit of error.

TWO AREAS OF DECEPTION

Human Deception

> ### *Rebellious People*

Men deceive others for many reasons, but financial gain and a desire for position and adoration are three of the main causes.

Titus 1:10 For there are many insubordinate, both idle talkers and deceivers, especially those of the circumcision.

Romans 16:18 For those who are such do not serve our Lord Jesus Christ, but their own belly, and by smooth words and flattering speech deceive the hearts of the simple.

> ### *Ananias and Sapphira*

Peter, through this gift, discerned that Ananias and Sapphira's hearts were filled with Satan's lies. They held back a portion of money which had been pledged to the ministry. Distinguishing between spirits insures the body of Christ against the infiltration of deceivers.

Acts 5:1-3 But a certain man named Ananias, with Sapphira his wife, sold a possession. And he kept back part of the proceeds, his wife also being aware of it, and brought a certain part and laid it at the apostles' feet.

But Peter said, "Ananias, why has Satan filled your heart to lie to the Holy Spirit and keep back part of the price of the land for yourself?"

➤ *Impostors*

2 Timothy 3:13 But evil men and impostors will grow worse and worse, deceiving and being deceived.

Satanic Deception

2 John 1:7 For many deceivers have gone out into the world who do not confess Jesus Christ as coming in the flesh. This is a deceiver and an antichrist.

Matthew 24:24 For false christs and false prophets will arise and show great signs and wonders, so as to deceive, if possible, even the elect.

Through the distinguishing between spirits, we can know when we are being deceived either by Satan through people or situations, or by people themselves. This revealed knowledge becomes our protection.

JESUS OPERATED IN DISTINGUISHING BETWEEN SPIRITS

"You Are the Christ"

We have two examples of statements made by Peter. One is of God the other of Satan. As Jesus operated in the distinguishing between spirits, we can see how we also need to operate in this gift.

Matthew 16:16,17 And Simon Peter answered and said, "You are the Christ, the Son of the living God."

Jesus answered and said to him, "Blessed are you, Simon Bar-Jonah, for flesh and blood has not revealed this to you, but My Father who is in heaven."

Peter's statement was not made out of human knowledge, but it was revealed by the Father.

Satan Rebuked

Soon after the above statement, Peter took it upon himself to rebuke Jesus saying that Jesus wasn't to suffer. We might argue that it was Peter's concern for Jesus which caused him to stop Jesus. In other words, his statement didn't seem wrong on the surface. But Jesus addressed Peter as Satan because Jesus discerned the spirit which was the source of Peter's statement.

Matthew 16:22,23 Then Peter took Him aside and began to rebuke Him, saying, "Far be it from You, Lord; this shall not happen to You!"

But He turned and said to Peter, "Get behind Me, Satan! You are an offense to Me, for you are not mindful of the things of God, but the things of men."

Deaf and Dumb Spirit

Jesus often ministered healing by speaking to the spirit causing the problem.

Mark 9:25b He rebuked the unclean spirit, saying to him, "You deaf and dumb spirit, I command you, come out of him, and enter him no more!"

OLD TESTAMENT EXAMPLE – DISTINGUISHING BETWEEN SPIRITS

Servant Sees Spirit World

Elisha prayed that his servant would see into the spirit realm.

2 Kings 6:16,17 So he answered, "Do not fear, for those who are with us are more than those who are with them."

And Elisha prayed, and said, "LORD, I pray, open his eyes that he may see." Then the LORD opened the eyes of the young man, and he saw. And behold, the mountain was full of horses and chariots of fire all around Elisha.

Anytime a person sees into the spirit world – revealing good or evil spirits, it's the distinguishing between spirits.

We should pray, like Elisha, that our own spiritual eyes will be opened.

Isaiah Saw

Isaiah 6:1 In the year that King Uzziah died, I saw the Lord sitting on a throne, high and lifted up, and the train of His robe filled the temple.

NEW TESTAMENT EXAMPLE – DISTINGUISHING BETWEEN SPIRITS

Paul and Slave Girl

➤ *Good Saying from Evil Spirit*

Acts 16:16-18 Now it happened, as we went to prayer, that a certain slave girl possessed with a spirit of divination met us, who brought her masters much profit by fortune-telling.

This girl followed Paul and us, and cried out, saying, "These men are the servants of the Most High God, who proclaim to us the way of salvation."

And this she did for many days. But Paul, greatly annoyed, turned and said to the spirit, "I command you in the name of Jesus Christ to come out of her." And he came out that very hour.

Was the divination spirit within this girl trying to cover its existence by giving a "good report." What the girl said was true.

We are told that Paul was troubled for several days. Why? Paul was waiting to know her spirit.

➢ *Motive*

It is very possible, the spirits within her were looking for accreditation by association.

THE GIFT OF DISTINGUISHING BETWEEN SPIRITS TODAY

Don't be Ignorant

Remember – God doesn't want us to be ignorant of the spirits around us – the spirits we are in business with – the spirits which exist in our area.

We cannot just think something is right, we must know which spirits are operating from God.

We don't know the spirit a person is operating in until God shows us.

1 John 4:6 We are of God. He who knows God hears us; he who is not of God does not hear us. By this we know the spirit of truth and the spirit of error.

We are of God and have the right to know the difference between the spirits of truth and the spirits of error.

Take Action

God doesn't reveal evil spirits to the believer without purpose. Whenever evil spirits are discerned, they should immediately be either bound or cast out depending on the circumstances.

Mark 16:17 And these signs will follow those who believe: in My name they will cast out demons; they will speak with new tongues ...

Luke 10:19,20 Behold, I give you the authority to trample on serpents and scorpions, and over all the power of the enemy, and nothing shall by any means hurt you. Nevertheless do not rejoice in this, that the spirits are subject to you, but rather rejoice because your names are written in heaven.

You have already been given power over the enemy. Jesus told us what to do.

➢ Cast out the demons

➢ Trample on serpents and scorpions

➢ Overcome all the power of the enemy

➢ Not to rejoice that spirits are subject to us – but that we are of God

DANGER OF WRONG MOTIVES

We are warned of the danger of trying to gain the gifts of the Holy Spirit through wrong motivation.

Simon

Acts 8:7-9 For unclean spirits, crying with a loud voice, came out of many who were possessed; and many who were paralyzed and lame were healed. And there was great joy in that city.

But there was a certain man called Simon, who previously practiced sorcery in the city and astonished the people of Samaria, claiming that he was someone great.

Acts 8:13,18-24 Then Simon himself also believed; and when he was baptized he continued with Philip, and was amazed, seeing the miracles and signs which were done.

➤ *Offered Money*

Now when Simon saw that through the laying on of the apostles' hands the Holy Spirit was given, he offered them money, Saying, "Give me this power also, that anyone on whom I lay hands may receive the Holy Spirit."

➤ *Denounced by Peter*

But Peter said to him, "Your money perish with you, because you thought that the gift of God could be purchased with money! You have neither part nor portion in this matter, for your heart is not right in the sight of God. Repent therefore of this your wickedness, and pray God if perhaps the thought of your heart may be forgiven you.

Peter discerned the spirit-being affecting Simon's action.

For I see that you are poisoned by bitterness and bound by iniquity."

Then Simon answered and said, "Pray to the Lord for me, that none of the things which you have spoken may come upon me."

Bar-Jesus

➤ *Opposed Apostles*

Acts 13:6-12 Now when they had gone through the island to Paphos, they found a certain sorcerer, a false prophet, a Jew whose name was Bar-Jesus, who was with the proconsul, Sergius Paulus, an intelligent man. This man called for Barnabas and Saul and sought to hear the word of God. But Elymas the sorcerer (for so his name is translated) withstood them, seeking to turn the proconsul away from the faith.

➤ *Clearly Identified*

Then Saul, who also is called Paul, filled with the Holy Spirit, looked intently at him and said, "O full of all deceit and all fraud, you son of the devil, you enemy of all righteousness, will you not cease perverting the straight ways of the Lord? And now, indeed, the hand of the Lord is upon you, and you shall be blind, not seeing the sun for a time."

➤ *Judgment*

And immediately a dark mist fell on him, and he went around seeking someone to lead him by the hand. Then the proconsul believed, when he saw what had been done, being astonished at the teaching of the Lord.

QUESTIONS FOR REVIEW

1. Explain the gift of distinguishing between spirits in your own words.

2. Why is the operation of this gift important to you?

3. Describe three areas of spirit activity which you may be involved with.

Lesson Nine

Revelation Gift

Word of Knowledge

1 Corinthians 12:8-10 To one there is given through the Spirit the message of wisdom, to another the message of knowledge by means of the same Spirit, to another faith by the same Spirit, to another gifts of healing by that one Spirit, to another miraculous powers, to another prophecy, to another distinguishing between spirits, to another speaking in different kinds of tongues, and to still another the interpretation of tongues.

Nine Gifts of the Spirit		
Vocal Inspiration	**Revelation**	**Power**
Tongues	Distinguishing Between Spirits	Gift of Faith
Interpretation of Tongues	↳ **Word of Knowledge**	Gifts of Healing
Prophecy	Word of Wisdom	Working of Miracles

THE WORD OF KNOWLEDGE

Definition

The word of knowledge is a supernatural revelation by the Holy Spirit of certain facts, present or past, about a person or situation, which were not learned through the natural mind. It will often interrupt the natural thoughts of our minds. It will come as a thought, a word, a name, a feeling, an impression, a vision or as an "inner knowing." Even as a word is a small part of a sentence, the word of knowledge is a small part of God's total knowledge of the situation.

The word of knowledge isn't an excuse for not spending time studying God's Word.

2 Timothy 2:15 Be diligent to present yourself approved to God, a worker who does not need to be ashamed, rightly dividing the word of truth.

The word of knowledge, however, isn't the knowledge which comes from years of walking with the Lord and spending time in His Word.

Four Kinds of Knowledge

➢ *Human*

Human knowledge is naturally acquired through education, scientific investigation, and life experiences. Much good has come through this area of knowledge. But without the knowledge of God, incomplete or erroneous conclusions have been made resulting in wrong thinking.

➤ *Evil Supernatural*

Knowledge of the supernatural which is of an evil source is learned by some through witchcraft, occult involvement, idol worship, religious deities, metaphysical investigation, and other satanic areas. This area of knowledge can be very enticing and must be completely rejected. It is forbidden by God.

➤ *Spiritual Knowledge*

The knowledge of spiritual areas begins at the moment we accept Jesus as our Savior.

John 17:3 And this is eternal life, that they may know You, the only true God, and Jesus Christ whom You have sent.

This knowledge increases through Bible study, teachings, praying, and communion with God.

➤ *Word of Knowledge*

Supernatural revelation from God of certain facts, present or past, which were not learned through the natural mind.

Purpose

God never intended for His people to live on the natural level. We are spirit-beings and must learn to operate in the realm of the Spirit for our protection, as well as those around us.

God desires to communicate with us through the word of knowledge for many reasons. One of the primary purposes is to aid and assist in perfecting the purposes of God in the midst of His people.

The word of knowledge will be revealed, delivered and ministered in such a way as to always bring glory to God, never to a man or woman. It will aid and assist them in ministry while always pointing to God as the source.

It helps us to minister with accuracy and effectiveness. It will warn of danger, bring encouragement, disclose sin and keep us "on track" in our daily life and ministry.

For Everyone

Is the word of knowledge to operate through all believers? Yes!

1 Corinthians 12:7 But the manifestation of the Spirit is given to each one for the profit of all.

➤ *Example of Ananias*

Ananias wasn't an apostle, pastor, evangelist or teacher. He was a layman, a believer. The Bible calls him a disciple.

Acts 9:10-12 Now there was a certain disciple at Damascus named Ananias; and to him the Lord said in a vision, "Ananias."

And he said, "Here I am, Lord."

So the Lord said to him, "Arise and go to the street called Straight, and inquire at the house of Judas for one called Saul of Tarsus, for behold, he is praying. And in a vision he has seen a man named Ananias coming in and putting his hand on him, so that he might receive his sight."

God told Ananias:

➤ The name of the street

➤ The name of Saul

➤ That Saul had been given a vision

The contents of that vision was both a word of knowledge and a word of wisdom. The knowledge was the facts. The wisdom was the revelation of what Ananias was to do and what would happen.

WORD OF KNOWLEDGE IN OPERATION

We may see something in the spirit around a person or place.

We may hear a word or phrase in our inner man.

We may feel in our own body a manifestation of something concerning another person.

The fact that we have received a word of knowledge doesn't mean that we are to act on it immediately. Often we need to wait for a word of wisdom to tell us how we are to proceed. At other times the word of knowledge and wisdom will operate simultaneously and allow immediate fulfillment of God's purpose.

A word of knowledge may be used by God to confront another person with a wrongful situation they are in, or of sin in their lives. Such words must be given in love, usually in private, and always when operating in the word of wisdom!

Warnings!

The Holy Spirit doesn't give words of knowledge to promote one person above others. Be careful of any "word of knowledge" which would tend to bring attention to self, or to build-up a certain ministry. God doesn't deal in "secrets."

Jesus never operated on His own initiative. He always had His Spirit tuned in to heaven. When He saw the Father do, or say, something, He would act on that word of knowledge or word of wisdom.

John 5:19 Then Jesus answered and said to them, "Most assuredly, I say to you, the Son can do nothing of Himself, but what He sees the Father do; for whatever He does, the Son also does in like manner."

Any "revelation gift" that adds facts to biblical incidents would be very suspect. A word of knowledge will always mirror the Word of God as written. The Holy Spirit being the author of the Word, will never alter, or change what He has written.

Any "fact" that would change or add to salvation or a knowledge of the Godhead must be rejected as not from God.

If the Spirit of God is moving in a certain area of thought or ministry during a meeting, there will not be a true word of knowledge which moves abruptly into a completely different area. God expects you to act on the revelation, but it must fit the flow, anointing and timing of each particular gathering.

We are expected to carry out the Holy Spirit's instructions in accordance to God's timing and His order. He is never the author of confusion.

EXAMPLES OF WORD OF KNOWLEDGE IN OLD TESTAMENT

Ahijah Warned of Deception

Ahijah the prophet was warned by God of a deception which was to come against him.

1 Kings 14:2-6 And Jeroboam said to his wife, "Please arise, and disguise yourself, that they may not recognize you as the wife of Jeroboam, and go to Shiloh. Indeed, Ahijah the prophet is there, who told me that I would be king over this people. Also take with you ten loaves, some cakes, and a jar of honey, and go to him; he will tell you what will become of the child."

And Jeroboam's wife did so; she arose and went to Shiloh, and came to the house of Ahijah. But Ahijah could not see, for his eyes were glazed by reason of his age. Now the LORD had said to Ahijah, "Here is the wife of Jeroboam, coming to ask you something about her son, for he is sick. Thus and thus you shall say to her;

for it will be, when she comes in, that she will pretend to be another woman."

And so it was, when Ahijah heard the sound of her footsteps as she came through the door, he said, "Come in, wife of Jeroboam. Why do you pretend to be another person? For I have been sent to you with bad news."

The word of knowledge and the word of wisdom were in operation when the Lord told him:

➢ Who she was – wife of Jeroboam

➢ Why she had come – to ask for son

➢ What he would say – thus you shall say

➢ What she would do – pretend to be another

Ahijah then proceeded to prophesy to her about the end of Jeroboam's reign. His word of knowledge concerning this deception gave his prophecy much more credence.

Elijah Encouraged

After the Prophet Elijah had called down the fire of God at Mount Carmel, Jezebel threatened his life. Elijah ran and then in the depth of discouragement he cried out to God.

➢ *Take my Life*

1 Kings 19:4,14 But he himself went a day's journey into the wilderness, and came and sat down under a broom tree. And he prayed that he might die, and said, "It is enough! Now, LORD, take my life, for I am no better than my fathers!"

➢ *I'm only One Left*

So he said, "I have been very zealous for the LORD God of hosts; because the children of Israel have forsaken Your covenant, torn down Your altars, and killed Your prophets with the sword. I alone am left; and they seek to take my life."

➢ *God Had 7,000*

God answered,

1 Kings 19:18 "Yet I have reserved seven thousand in Israel, all whose knees have not bowed to Baal, and every mouth that has not kissed him."

Gehazi Exposed

The word of knowledge operated more times through Elisha than any other person recorded in the Old Testament.

After Naaman was healed he offered to reward Elisha two times but Elisha refused any type of payment, or showing of gratitude.

➤ *Lied to Naaman*

2 Kings 5:20-27 But Gehazi, the servant of Elisha the man of God, said, "Look, my master has spared Naaman this Syrian, while not receiving from his hands what he brought; but as the LORD lives, I will run after him and take something from him."

So Gehazi pursued Naaman. When Naaman saw him running after him, he got down from the chariot to meet him, and said, "Is all well?"

And he said, "All is well. My master has sent me, saying, 'Indeed, just now two young men of the sons of the prophets have come to me from the mountains of Ephraim. Please give them a talent of silver and two changes of garments.' "

So Naaman said, "Please, take two talents." And he urged him, and bound two talents of silver in two bags, with two changes of garments, and handed them to two of his servants; and they carried them on ahead of him.

➤ *Hid Stolen Items*

When he came to the citadel, he took them from their hand, and stored them away in the house; then he let the men go, and they departed.

➤ *Lied to Elisha*

Now he went in and stood before his master. And Elisha said to him, "Where did you go, Gehazi?" And he said, "Your servant did not go anywhere."

Elisha had supernaturally seen, (an operation of the word of knowledge), all that Gehazi did. He described in detail what he saw through this gift.

➤ *Result Was Leprosy*

Then he said to him, "Did not my heart go with you when the man turned back from his chariot to meet you? Is it time to receive money and to receive clothing, olive groves and vineyards, sheep and oxen, male and female servants? Therefore the leprosy of Naaman shall cling to you and your descendants forever." And he went out from his presence leprous, as white as snow.

Warning of Enemy's Plan

Elisha was so in tune with God's voice that the Syrian king began to search for the traitor in his midst. Then his servant told him, Elisha, the prophet, tells the king of Israel the very words you speak in your bedroom!

2 Kings 6:9-12 **And the man of God sent to the king of Israel, saying, "Beware that you do not pass this place, for the Syrians are coming down there."**

Then the king of Israel sent someone to the place of which the man of God had told him. Thus he warned him, and he was watchful there, not just once or twice.

Therefore the heart of the king of Syria was greatly troubled by this thing; and he called his servants and said to them, "Will you not show me which of us is for the king of Israel?"

And one of his servants said, "None, my lord, O king; but Elisha, the prophet who is in Israel, tells the king of Israel the words that you speak in your bedroom."

WORD OF KNOWLEDGE IN LIFE OF JESUS

When we study the life of Jesus it's easy to think, "Oh, He could do that. He operated as God." But Jesus laid aside His abilities as God and walked on the face of this earth exactly like Adam was created to walk. He is our example. The things which He did we are to do also! He operated on this earth in the power of the Holy Spirit the same as believers today are to do.

Samaritan Woman

While Jesus was talking to the woman at the well, He received a word of knowledge concerning her husbands. This knowledge of something which He couldn't have known in the natural led to the salvation of many in that village. It is important to notice that even though Jesus knew something which was condemning, He didn't use that knowledge to condemn. Through the word of wisdom, He used the knowledge to bring her to salvation.

John 4:16-18,39-42 **Jesus said to her, "Go, call your husband, and come here."**

The woman answered and said, "I have no husband."

➤ *"You Have Had Five"*

Jesus said to her, "You have well said, 'I have no husband,' for you have had five husbands, and the one whom you now have is not your husband; in that you spoke truly."

And many of the Samaritans of that city believed in Him because of the word of the woman who testified, "He told me all that I ever did."

➤ *Result – Many Believed*

So when the Samaritans had come to Him, they urged Him to stay with them; and He stayed there two days. And many more believed because of His own word.

Then they said to the woman, "Now we believe, not because of what you said, for we have heard for ourselves and know that this is indeed the Christ, the Savior of the world."

Blind Man

Jesus knew that the cause of the man's blindness wasn't due to his sin or that of his father. There is no way in the natural that He could have known this. It was through the word of knowledge.

John 9:3 Jesus answered, "Neither this man nor his parents sinned, but that the works of God should be revealed in him."

To Pay Taxes

When it was time to pay the Roman tax Jesus instructed Peter to catch a fish, open its mouth and take out the coin they needed. Again, there was no way in the natural that He could have known this.

Matthew 17:27 Nevertheless, lest we offend them, go to the sea, cast in a hook, and take the fish that comes up first. And when you have opened its mouth, you will find a piece of money; take that and give it to them for Me and you.

At Passover

Jesus knew the disciples would meet a man carrying a jar of water. They were to follow him to the house and that this house would have an upper room furnished for them to use.

Luke 22:10-12 And He said to them, "Behold, when you have entered the city, a man will meet you carrying a pitcher of water; follow him into the house which he enters. Then you shall say to the master of the house, 'The Teacher says to you, "Where is the guest room in which I may eat the Passover with My disciples?"' Then he will show you a large, furnished upper room; there make ready."

Who Betrayer Was

Jesus knew who would betray Him.

John 13:26 Jesus answered, "It is he to whom I shall give a piece of bread when I have dipped it." And having dipped the bread, He gave it to Judas Iscariot, the son of Simon.

EXAMPLES IN THE NEW TESTAMENT

Cornelius

Cornelius received instructions through a vision. The instructions were that he was to call for Peter who would tell him what he should do.

Acts 10:1-6 There was a certain man in Caesarea called Cornelius, a centurion of what was called the Italian Regiment, a devout man and one who feared God with all his household, who gave alms generously to the people, and prayed to God always. About the ninth hour of the day he saw clearly in a vision an angel of God coming in and saying to him, "Cornelius!"

And when he observed him, he was afraid, and said, "What is it, lord?"

So he said to him, "Your prayers and your alms have come up for a memorial before God. Now send men to Joppa, and send for Simon whose surname is Peter. He is lodging with Simon, a tanner, whose house is by the sea. He will tell you what you must do."

Word of knowledge told him:

➤ Man was named Simon Peter,

➤ Stayed with Simon the tanner,

➤ House was by the sea.

The word of knowledge was in operation in giving facts, but the word of wisdom was operating in telling him what to do.

Peter

Peter wouldn't have gone to a Gentiles' home without the supernatural intervention of God in a vision.

Acts 10:17-19 Now while Peter wondered within himself what this vision which he had seen meant, behold, the men who had been sent from Cornelius had made inquiry for Simon's house, and stood before the gate. And they called and asked whether Simon, whose surname was Peter, was lodging there.

➤ *Word of Knowledge*

While Peter thought about the vision, the Spirit said to him, "Behold, three men are seeking you."

Peter wondered about what he had seen in the vision. It went against everything he had been taught. But God immediately confirmed the vision with the coming of the men. In this situation the word of knowledge opened the whole Gentile world to the gospel of Jesus Christ.

Acts 10:44 While Peter was still speaking these words, the Holy Spirit fell upon all those who heard the word.

Because Cornelius prayed the word of God's knowledge could come.

Paul

In Lystra Paul looked and saw the faith of an impotent man. This was the word of knowledge in action.

Acts 14:8-10 And in Lystra a certain man without strength in his feet was sitting, a cripple from his mother's womb, who had never walked. This man heard Paul speaking. Paul, observing him intently and seeing that he had faith to be healed, Said with a loud voice, "Stand up straight on your feet!" And he leaped and walked.

QUESTIONS FOR REVIEW

1. What kind of knowledge is the word of knowledge? Compare it with other areas of knowledge.

2. How may a person receive a word of knowledge?

3. Give an illustration from your own experience of the word of knowledge working through you.

Lesson Ten

Revelation Gift
Word of Wisdom

1 Corinthians 12:8-10 To one there is given through the Spirit the message of wisdom, to another the message of knowledge by means of the same Spirit, to another faith by the same Spirit, to another gifts of healing by that one Spirit, to another miraculous powers, to another prophecy, to another distinguishing between spirits, to another speaking in different kinds of tongues, and to still another the interpretation of tongues.

Nine Gifts of he Spirit		
Vocal Inspiration	**Revelation**	**Power**
Tongues	Distinguishing Between Spirits	Gift of Faith
Interpretation of Tongues	Word of Knowledge	Gifts of Healing
Prophecy	✍ **Word of Wisdom**	Working of Miracles

THE WORD OF WISDOM

Definition

The gift of the word of wisdom is a supernatural revelation by the Holy Spirit giving the believer God's wisdom to proceed on a course of action based on natural or supernatural knowledge. It reveals God's plan and purpose for our life and ministry. It reveals what God purposes to be done immediately, in a short while or in the near or distant future. It reveals what an individual or corporate gathering should do and how to proceed in God's will. The Word of wisdom often operates and flows with the word of knowledge.

Comes in Many Forms

The word of wisdom can come in many forms:

➢ An inner voice,

➢ Through a vision when awake,

➢ Through a dream when asleep,

➢ Through other persons operating in the gifts of tongues and interpretation of tongues, or the gift of prophecy.

Not Natural Wisdom

The word of wisdom isn't a natural gift of wisdom. It's a word, or phrase, a part not the whole.

1 Corinthians 13:9 For we know in part and we prophesy in part.

When the word of wisdom begins to operate, only a portion of God's wisdom is shared with the believer. God will reveal a limited portion of His foreknowledge to the believer through the spirit of man. It is often given quickly to the believer interrupting the natural thought patterns. The natural thoughts of man are momentarily blended and/or infused with the thoughts of God. The result is the believer suddenly becomes aware of God's plan and purpose and how to proceed in the perfect will of God.

It will come as an impression or a vision in which we will see ourselves in the spirit doing something in a certain way before we do it.

1 Corinthians 2:11-13 For what man knows the things of a man except the spirit of the man which is in him? Even so no one knows the things of God except the Spirit of God.

Now we have received, not the spirit of the world, but the Spirit who is from God, that we might know the things that have been freely given to us by God. These things we also speak, not in words which man's wisdom teaches but which the Holy Spirit teaches, comparing spiritual things with spiritual.

Ask for Wisdom

When God said that any of us could ask for wisdom He was speaking of supernatural wisdom to operate in the natural realm.

James 1:5 If any of you lacks wisdom, let him ask of God, who gives to all liberally and without reproach, and it will be given to him.

Seek Wisdom

When we allow the Holy Spirit to operate through our lives in words of wisdom, we can move from the natural realm into the supernatural realm. As we pray for ourselves and for others, we can receive supernatural wisdom which reveals to us how to pray and what to say.

Be Saturated in Word

The word of wisdom should not be confused with natural, or learned wisdom. It isn't an excuse for not striving to gain wisdom as we are instructed throughout the book of Proverbs.

Proverbs 2:1-6 My son, if you receive my words, and treasure my commands within you, so that you incline your ear to wisdom, and apply your heart to understanding; yes, if you cry out for discernment, and lift up your voice for understanding, if you seek her as silver, and search for her as for hidden treasures; then you will understand the fear of the LORD, and find the knowledge of God.

Joshua was told that he was to meditate on the Word, both day and night. By so doing we lay a solid Word foundation from which the gift of the word of wisdom can operate.

Joshua 1:8 This Book of the Law shall not depart from your mouth, but you shall meditate in it day and night, that you may observe to do according to all that is written in it. For then you will make your way prosperous, and then you will have good success.

Purpose

The word of wisdom is given for protection and for instruction.

The word of wisdom often will reveal to us how to apply knowledge revealed through a word of knowledge or distinguishing between spirits. It may give an insight of how to pray in a certain situation. It may give us the "key" to help a person we are praying with.

The believer will suddenly hear new, fresh, creative words or phrases in his spirit. These words will most often interrupt the natural thought processes as if they are injected into the mind spontaneously. This is the work of the Holy Spirit causing the believer to be aware of the will of God for the situation. It can happen anytime, anywhere, sometimes when least expected. That is how you know it's the Holy Spirit and not yourself thinking these things. It comes unexpectedly. But, these revelations are always welcomed to help us carry out God's plan and purpose for the situation.

RECEIVING WORD OF WISDOM

All gifts of the Spirit are received through faith. If we aren't operating in a certain gift, we can ask God to release any of the gifts through us.

Matthew 7:7,8,11 Ask, and it will be given to you; seek, and you will find; knock, and it will be opened to you. For everyone who asks receives, and he who seeks finds, and to him who knocks it will be opened.

If you then, being evil, know how to give good gifts to your children, how much more will your Father who is in heaven give good things to those who ask Him!

Steps to receiving the word of wisdom:

➢ Pray and ask God for the gift of wisdom to be manifested in your life.

➢ In faith expect God to act.

➢ Act on any leading, no matter how foolish it may seem to you.

➢ Watch for confirmation.

COMPARISONS BETWEEN WORDS OF KNOWLEDGE AND WISDOM

The difference between the word of knowledge and the word of wisdom is that the word of knowledge deals in facts either present or past. The word of wisdom deals with understanding how those facts should be acted upon according to God's best plan.

Since the word of knowledge deals with facts in the past or present, it does not deal with the future. The word of wisdom deals with the future and supernatural wisdom in acting out God's will as revealed, before it happens.

Gifts Operate Together

For the purpose of studying, and since they are listed separately in Corinthians we study these two gifts separately. However very often they operate so closely together that it's difficult to separate them.

➢ *John at Patmos*

While John was exiled on the isle of Patmos, he had no present knowledge of the churches of Asia. God appeared to him and gave him the present condition of the churches when he wrote letters to seven of them. That was the operation of the gift of the word of knowledge since it dealt with facts. Then God proceeded to tell him what each of the churches would do in the future. That was the operation of the word of wisdom.

➢ *Ananias*

Ananias, as we discussed in Lesson Nine was given many facts when God told him to go to Saul and lay hands on him. However, when Ananias was still afraid to go to him, God reassured him by telling him what He had chosen for Saul to do and the things which would happen to Saul in the future. That was the operation of the word of wisdom.

JESUS OPERATED IN WORD OF WISDOM

It is important to remember when we are studying the life of Jesus that Jesus emptied Himself of His divine attributes and operated on this earth exactly like men were created to operate.

Woman at Well

Jesus received a word of knowledge that the woman at the well had five husbands and was living in adultery with another man. Instead of acting on this knowledge in the natural, He received a word of wisdom and acted by supernatural revelation. Instead of calling her an adulteress and calling for her to be stoned according the law, He acted according to the word of wisdom which He had received. (John 4:16-29)

By operating in the word of wisdom, we too will be much more effective in our ministry.

Lazarus

When Jesus heard of the sickness of Lazarus, He immediately knew this death would bring glory to God by a resurrection.

John 11:4,14,17,23 When Jesus heard that, He said, "This sickness is not unto death, but for the glory of God, that the Son of God may be glorified through it."

Then Jesus said to them plainly, "Lazarus is dead."

So when Jesus came, He found that he had already been in the tomb four days.

Jesus said to her, "Your brother will rise again."

Rich Young Man

When the rich young man ran to Jesus, he asked Him,

Matthew 19:16b,17,21 "Good Teacher, what good thing shall I do that I may have eternal life?"

Jesus didn't answer his question. Instead, He went to the real problem.

So He said to him, "Why do you call Me good? No one is good but One, that is, God. But if you want to enter into life, keep the commandments."

And then Jesus listed six of the ten commandments. The young man insisted that he had done these from his youth. And then Jesus answered,

"If you want to be perfect, go, sell what you have and give to the poor, and you will have treasure in heaven; and come, follow Me."

How did Jesus know that the real problem lay in the love and attachment this man had for his possessions? Through the operation of the word of knowledge.

How did He know the best way to approach the problem? Through the operation of the word of wisdom.

Warned of Persecutions

Jesus warned the disciples of persecutions which were going to come, but with the warning, He promised them supernatural wisdom.

Luke 21:12-15 But before all these things, they will lay their hands on you and persecute you, delivering you up to the synagogues and prisons, and you will be brought before kings and rulers for My name's sake.

But it will turn out for you as an occasion for testimony. Therefore settle it in your hearts not to meditate beforehand on what you will answer; for I will give you a mouth and wisdom which all your adversaries will not be able to contradict or resist.

EXAMPLES IN OLD TESTAMENT

Hezekiah

Hezekiah's life was lengthened.

2 Kings 20:1-6 In those days Hezekiah was sick and near death. And Isaiah the prophet, the son of Amoz, went to him and said to him, "Thus says the LORD: 'Set your house in order, for you shall die, and not live.' "

Then he turned his face toward the wall, and prayed to the LORD, saying, "Remember now, O LORD, I pray, how I have walked before You in truth and with a loyal heart, and have done what was good in Your sight." And Hezekiah wept bitterly.

Then it happened, before Isaiah had gone out into the middle court, that the word of the LORD came to him, saying, Return and tell Hezekiah the leader of My people, 'Thus says the LORD, the God of David your father: "I have heard your prayer, I have seen your tears; surely I will heal you. On the third day you shall go up to the house of the LORD. And I will add to your days fifteen years. I will deliver you and this city from the hand of the king of Assyria; and I will defend this city for My own sake, and for the sake of My servant David." '

Coming Flood

The revelation to Noah of the coming great flood saved the human race and the animals.

Genesis 6:12,13 So God looked upon the earth, and indeed it was corrupt; for all flesh had corrupted their way on the earth. And God said to Noah, "The end of all flesh has come before Me, for

the earth is filled with violence through them; and behold, I will destroy them with the earth."

God's Covenant

Sometimes the word of wisdom is unconditional. An example of this was the covenant which God made with Noah.

Genesis 9:12-16 And God said: "This is the sign of the covenant which I make between Me and you, and every living creature that is with you, for perpetual generations: I set My rainbow in the cloud, and it shall be for the sign of the covenant between Me and the earth. It shall be, when I bring a cloud over the earth, that the rainbow shall be seen in the cloud; and I will remember My covenant which is between Me and you and every living creature of all flesh; the waters shall never again become a flood to destroy all flesh. The rainbow shall be in the cloud, and I will look on it to remember the everlasting covenant between God and every living creature of all flesh that is on the earth."

Lot Warned

Sometimes the word of wisdom is conditional and this is an example of such. Lot was warned to leave Sodom and since he heeded that warning his life was spared. Others didn't heed the warnings, disobeyed and were lost.

Genesis 19:12-16 Then the men said to Lot, "Have you anyone else here? Son-in-law, your sons, your daughters, and whomever you have in the city–take them out of this place! For we will destroy this place, because the outcry against them has grown great before the face of the LORD, and the LORD has sent us to destroy it."

So Lot went out and spoke to his sons-in-law, who had married his daughters, and said, "Get up, get out of this place; for the LORD will destroy this city!" But to his sons-in-law he seemed to be joking.

When the morning dawned, the angels urged Lot to hurry, saying, "Arise, take your wife and your two daughters who are here, lest you be consumed in the punishment of the city." And while he lingered, the men took hold of his hand, his wife's hand, and the hands of his two daughters, the LORD being merciful to him, and they brought him out and set him outside the city.

Daniel

Nebuchadnezzar had a dream and his spirit was troubled, but he forgot the dream. Then he demanded the wise men tell him the dream and also the interpretation. If they couldn't do this, all of the "wise men" in the land were to be killed. This included Daniel. Daniel received a night vision which told him both the dream and the interpretation.

Daniel 2:19 Then the secret was revealed to Daniel in a night vision. So Daniel blessed the God of heaven.

EXAMPLES IN THE NEW TESTAMENT

Coming Famine

Believers were warned of a coming famine and relief was sent.

Acts 11:28-30 Then one of them, named Agabus, stood up and showed by the Spirit that there was going to be a great famine throughout all the world, which also happened in the days of Claudius Caesar.

Then the disciples, each according to his ability, determined to send relief to the brethren dwelling in Judea. This they also did, and sent it to the elders by the hands of Barnabas and Saul.

Paul's Imprisonment

Agabus foretold Paul's imprisonment.

Acts 21:10,11 And as we stayed many days, a certain prophet named Agabus came down from Judea. When he had come to us, he took Paul's belt, bound his own hands and feet, and said, "Thus says the Holy Spirit, 'So shall the Jews at Jerusalem bind the man who owns this belt, and deliver him into the hands of the Gentiles.' "

Shipwreck

Before sailing for Crete, Paul was warned of a shipwreck with much loss of life and property. He delivered the warning, but since they didn't heed it, the ship, provisions, and cargo were lost.

Acts 27:10,21-26 Saying, "Men, I perceive that this voyage will end with disaster and much loss, not only of the cargo and ship, but also our lives."

They didn't heed this first warning.

But after long abstinence from food, then Paul stood in the midst of them and said, "Men, you should have listened to me, and not have sailed from Crete and incurred this disaster and loss. And now I urge you to take heart, for there will be no loss of life among you, but only of the ship. For there stood by me this night an angel of the God to whom I belong and whom I serve, saying, 'Do not be afraid, Paul; you must be brought before Caesar; and indeed God has granted you all those who sail with you.' Therefore take heart, men, for I believe God that it will be just as it was told me. However, we must run aground on a certain island."

Even after Paul gave them these words of wisdom some started to disobey.

Acts 27:30,31,44 And as the sailors were seeking to escape from the ship, when they had let down the skiff into the sea, under pretense of putting out anchors from the prow, Paul said to the centurion and the soldiers, "Unless these men stay in the ship, you cannot be saved."

And the rest, some on boards and some on broken pieces of the ship. And so it was that they all escaped safely to land.

USED TO SET APART FOR SPECIAL MINISTRY

Ananias Sent to Saul

The Lord spoke to Ananias and told him to go and lay hands on Saul that he might receive his sight and from that time Saul became Paul and was set apart to take the message of salvation to the Gentiles.

Acts 9:11-15 So the Lord said to him, "Arise and go to the street called Straight, and inquire at the house of Judas for one called Saul of Tarsus, for behold, he is praying. And in a vision he has seen a man named Ananias coming in and putting his hand on him, so that he might receive his sight."

Then Ananias answered, "Lord, I have heard from many about this man, how much harm he has done to Your saints in Jerusalem. And here he has authority from the chief priests to bind all who call on Your name."

But the Lord said to him, "Go, for he is a chosen vessel of Mine to bear My name before Gentiles, kings, and the children of Israel."

Saul and Barnabas

Saul and Barnabas were set apart for a special work at the instructions of the Holy Ghost.

Acts 13:1-4 Now in the church that was at Antioch there were certain prophets and teachers: Barnabas, Simeon who was called Niger, Lucius of Cyrene, Manaen who had been brought up with Herod the tetrarch, and Saul. As they ministered to the Lord and fasted, the Holy Spirit said, "Now separate to Me Barnabas and Saul for the work to which I have called them."

Then, having fasted and prayed, and laid hands on them, they sent them away. So, being sent out by the Holy Spirit, they went down to Seleucia, and from there they sailed to Cyprus.

Apostle John

The apostle John was caught up in the Spirit on the Lord's Day, and the entire book of Revelation flashed before him.

Revelation 1:10 I was in the Spirit on the Lord's Day, and I heard behind me a loud voice, as of a trumpet ...

4:2 Immediately I was in the Spirit; and behold, a throne set in heaven, and One sat on the throne.

17:3 So he carried me away in the Spirit into the wilderness. And I saw a woman sitting on a scarlet beast which was full of names of blasphemy, having seven heads and ten horns.

21:10 And he carried me away in the Spirit to a great and high mountain, and showed me the great city, the holy Jerusalem, descending out of heaven from God.

When John knew facts about the actual seven churches, he was operating in the word of knowledge.

When he knew of things to come, he was operating in the word of wisdom.

QUESTIONS FOR REVIEW

1. Write in your own words what the word of wisdom is.

2. Give an example of Jesus operating in the word of knowledge and the word of wisdom.

3. How do the word of knowledge and wisdom operate together? Give an example from your own life experiences.

Power Gift of Faith

1 Corinthians 12:9-11 To another faith by the same Spirit, to another gifts of healings by the same Spirit, To another the working of miracles, to another prophecy, to another discerning of spirits, to another different kinds of tongues, to another the interpretation of tongues. But one and the same Spirit works all these things, distributing to each one individually as He wills.

Nine Gifts of the Spirit		
Vocal Inspiration	**Revelation**	**Power**
Tongues	Distinguishing Between Spirits	✥ **Gift of Faith**
Interpretation Of Tongues	Word of Knowledge	Gifts of Healing
Prophecy	Word of Wisdom	Working of Miracles

FAITH, WORKING OF MIRACLES, GIFTS OF HEALING

Introduction

There are three gifts of vocal inspiration – tongues, interpretation, and prophecy. These gifts are the manifestation of God speaking through us.

There are three gifts of revelation – distinguishing between spirits, word of knowledge, and word of wisdom. These gifts are the manifestation of God revealing things to us; things of the natural world or of the spirit realms.

Finally, there are three gifts of power – gift of faith, workings of miracles, and gifts of healing. The power gifts are manifested by God releasing His supernatural faith or power to flow through us. The three power gifts are the gift of faith, the gifts of healing, and the working of miracles.

God desires to speak to the people of this world. Most of the time He speaks through His believers. God wants to reveal many things to this world. Again, He wants to do this through believers. God yearns to reach the needs of this generation, but He works through His people.

For all Believers

Each of the gifts of the Spirit are a manifestation of the Spirit, nine separate ways in which He operates through the body of Christ.

One Gift or All

There has been teaching in the past that each believer is to operate in one gift, or maybe two. To accept this teaching, we must ask ourselves one question, "Why would the Holy Spirit reveal through a revelation gift the presence of a demonic spirit of cancer but deny us His power through one of the power gifts to cast that spirit out?"

Limited by Ourselves

The operation of the gifts of the Holy Spirit in our lives is limited only by ourselves. What are we willing to allow God to do through us? How much time are we willing to give to Him? How clean is the vessel we present to Him for His use?

1 Corinthians 12:4 *(Amplified)* **Now there are distinctive varieties and distributions of endowments [extraordinary powers distinguishing certain Christians, due to the power of divine grace operating in their souls by the Holy Spirit] and they vary, but the (Holy) Spirit remains the same.**

Gifts Flow Together

As we have studied before, each group of gifts works closely together. We are to speak in tongues when we receive the baptism in the Holy Spirit. That equips us to operate in the first gift. Then we are to pray for the gift of interpretation. That is the second gift. Then we are to desire to prophesy. That is the third gift.

Then we move into the second group of gifts, the gifts of revelation. Through these, God reveals to us many things. One area of revealed knowledge has to do with needs in our life or the lives of those about us. Then we move into the power gifts which are a releasing of God's power to meet those needs.

GIFT OF FAITH

Definition

The gift of faith is a supernatural faith for a specific time and purpose. It is a gift of power to accomplish a certain task in whatever situation we are in at that particular time.

The gift of faith is given when needed for a specific task immediately or in the very near future. When the word of wisdom is given telling us how a task should be done, it will spark the gift of faith into operation to boldly carry out the task according to what God has already planned.

How Received

The gift of faith is received by the operation of the revelation gifts. Supernatural faith comes upon the believer when the gift of the word of wisdom reveals a demonstration of God's power which is about to be manifested. It releases us to boldly act upon the revelation which we have just received.

How Manifested

Often the supernatural gift of faith is involved in the operation of the power gifts. It may be manifested in a powerful commanding sentence such as Jesus said to the storm, "Peace, be still!" or as He said, "Lazarus come forth!"

Upon receiving a revelation of what God wants done through the word of wisdom, the gift of faith will come upon the believer to finish the task. This special faith is realized when the plan of how to proceed is revealed by a word of wisdom. This releases the believer to boldly act on what has been given to him by God.

It is a time in the believer's life when he's not striving to believe. He knows what God's Word says, what God's will is, and that he has the supernatural power of God abiding in himself to bring a thing to pass. When the gift of faith is present the words which are spoken are directly inspired by the Holy Spirit and have the same authority as if God were speaking them. The results of the gift of faith may be a gift of working miracles or of healings.

Response to Gift of Faith

There can be many responses to the gift of faith.

> ➤ It brings glory to God.

> ➤ It causes others to believe in God.

> ➤ It brings amazement and fear.

The reality of a living God involved in the affairs of men is demonstrated.

FOUR KINDS OF FAITH

Saving Faith

The faith by which we accept Jesus as our Savior is a gift from God which comes through hearing the Word of God.

Ephesians 2:8 For by grace you have been saved through faith, and that not of yourselves; it is the gift of God ...

Fruit of Faith

Faithfulness is listed as one of the fruits of the Spirit. It is a faith which grows in the life of a Christian to establish him in spiritual character.

Galatians 5:22,23 But the fruit of the Spirit is love, joy, peace, longsuffering, kindness, goodness, faithfulness, gentleness, self-control. Against such there is no law.

General Faith

There is a general, every day type of faith which comes through knowing God, knowing His Word and believing. It is having faith that what He has said He will do. This faith is strengthened every time we pray and receive the answer to that prayer.

Mark 11:24 Therefore I say to you, whatever things you ask when you pray, believe that you receive them, and you will have them.

Gift of Faith

The gift of faith is a supernatural faith for a specific time and purpose.

EXAMPLES OF GIFT OF FAITH FROM JESUS' MINISTRY

Resurrection Faith

Jesus operated often in the gift of faith. The following are just a few of the times.

➤ *Raises Dead Man*

Luke 7:12-15a And when He came near the gate of the city, behold, a dead man was being carried out, the only son of his mother; and she was a widow. And a large crowd from the city was with her.

When the Lord saw her, He had compassion on her and said to her, "Do not weep."

Then He came and touched the open coffin, and those who carried him stood still. And He said, "Young man, I say to you, arise."

And he who was dead sat up and began to speak.

➤ *Lazarus*

Even as Jesus was told of the sickness of Lazarus, He knew that Lazarus' death and resurrection would be for a time of teaching on His own death and resurrection.

John 11:43b,44 ... He cried with a loud voice, "Lazarus, come forth!"

And he who had died came out bound hand and foot with grave-clothes, and his face was wrapped with a cloth. Jesus said to them, "Loose him, and let him go."

➤ *For His Own Resurrection*

The ultimate gift of faith was that of Jesus laying down His life to pay the penalty for the sins of all mankind and knowing that He would be resurrected.

John 11:25,26 Jesus said to her, "I am the resurrection and the life. He who believes in Me, though he may die, he shall live. And whoever lives and believes in Me shall never die. Do you believe this?"

Miracle Working Faith

➤ *Great Storm*

Mark 4:37,38 And a great windstorm arose, and the waves beat into the boat, so that it was already filling. But He was in the stern, asleep on a pillow. And they awoke Him and said to Him, "Teacher, do You not care that we are perishing?"

Then He arose and rebuked the wind, and said to the sea, "Peace, be still!" And the wind ceased and there was a great calm.

➤ *Walked on Water*

We often overlook the fact that Jesus, as a man, walked on the water. He operated on this earth as a man, not as God. Too often we look at Peter as a symbol of failure in this incident. It would be good for us to remember that Peter did just as Jesus did. He accomplished the "works of Jesus" on this occasion, even if only for a short time.

Matthew 14:25-32 Now in the fourth watch of the night Jesus went to them, walking on the sea. And when the disciples saw Him walking on the sea, they were troubled, saying, "It is a ghost!" And they cried out for fear.

But immediately Jesus spoke to them, saying, "Be of good cheer! It is I; do not be afraid."

And Peter answered Him and said, "Lord, if it is You, command me to come to You on the water."

So He said, "Come." And when Peter had come down out of the boat, he walked on the water to go to Jesus.

But when he saw that the wind was boisterous, he was afraid; and beginning to sink he cried out, saying, "Lord, save me!"

And immediately Jesus stretched out His hand and caught him, and said to him, "O you of little faith, why did you doubt?"

And when they got into the boat, the wind ceased.

GIFT OF FAITH IN SPEAKING GOD'S JUDGMENTS

Judgment

The gift of faith can operate in a seemingly destructive way for the protection of the body of Christ. Perhaps, the body of Christ because of sin in their lives, or fear of what people will say, or because of feelings of inadequacy has been reluctant to operate in these areas. Without the gifts of revelation operating in our lives it's impossible to operate in the gift of faith in the following manner.

➢ *By Jesus*

Jesus cursed the fig tree.

Matthew 21:19 And seeing a fig tree by the road, He came to it and found nothing on it but leaves, and said to it, "Let no fruit grow on you ever again." And immediately the fig tree withered away.

➢ *By Peter*

After Ananias had dropped dead, Peter spoke a curse on Sapphira as the gift of faith was released by a word of wisdom.

Acts 5:9-11 Then Peter said to her, "How is it that you have agreed together to test the Spirit of the Lord? Look, the feet of those who have buried your husband are at the door, and they will carry you out."

Then immediately she fell down at his feet and breathed her last. And the young men came in and found her dead, and carrying her out, buried her by her husband. So great fear came upon all the church and upon all who heard these things.

➢ *By Paul*

Acts 13:8-12 But Elymas the sorcerer (for so his name is translated) withstood them, seeking to turn the proconsul away from the faith.

Then Saul, who also is called Paul, filled with the Holy Spirit, looked intently at him and said, "O full of all deceit and all fraud, you son of the devil, you enemy of all righteousness, will you not cease perverting the straight ways of the Lord? And now, indeed, the hand of the Lord is upon you, and you shall be blind, not seeing the sun for a time." And immediately a dark mist fell on him, and he went around seeking someone to lead him by the hand.

Then the proconsul believed, when he saw what had been done, being astonished at the teaching of the Lord.

GIFT OF FAITH PROVIDES PROTECTION

David and Goliath

1 Samuel 17:32,38-40,45-49 Then David said to Saul, "Let no man's heart fail because of him; your servant will go and fight with this Philistine."

➤ *Man's Methods Laid Aside*

So Saul clothed David with his armor, and he put a bronze helmet on his head; he also clothed him with a coat of mail. And David fastened his sword to his armor, and he tried to walk, for he had not tested them. And David said to Saul, "I cannot walk with these, for I have not tested them."

So David took them off. Then he took his staff in his hand; and he chose for himself five smooth stones from the brook, and put them in a shepherd's bag, in a pouch which he had, and his sling was in his hand. And he drew near to the Philistine.

➤ *Gift of Faith*
  Word of Wisdom

Then David said to the Philistine, "You come to me with a sword, with a spear, and with a javelin. But I come to you in the name of the LORD of hosts, the God of the armies of Israel, whom you have defied. This day the LORD will deliver you into my hand, and I will strike you and take your head from you. And this day I will give the carcasses of the camp of the Philistines to the birds of the air and the wild beasts of the earth, that all the earth may know that there is a God in Israel. Then all this assembly shall know that the LORD does not save with sword and spear; for the battle is the Lord's, and He will give you into our hands."

➤ *Faith Brings Victory*

And it was so, when the Philistine arose and came and drew near to meet David, that David hastened and ran toward the army to meet the Philistine. Then David put his hand in his bag and took out a stone; and he slung it and struck the Philistine in his forehead, so that the stone sank into his forehead, and he fell on his face to the earth.

Daniel

➤ *King's Statement of Faith*

Daniel 6:16-22 So the king gave the command, and they brought Daniel and cast him into the den of lions. But the king spoke, saying to Daniel, "Your God, whom you serve continually, He will deliver you."

Then a stone was brought and laid on the mouth of the den, and the king sealed it with his own signet ring and with the signets of his lords, that the purpose concerning Daniel might not be changed.

Now the king went to his palace and spent the night fasting; and no musicians were brought before him. Also his sleep went from him. Then the king arose very early in the morning and went in haste to the den of lions. And when he came to the den, he cried out with a lamenting voice to Daniel. The king spoke, saying to Daniel, "Daniel, servant of the living God, has your God, whom you serve continually, been able to deliver you from the lions?"

➤ *Victory*

Then Daniel said to the king, "O king, live forever! My God sent His angel and shut the lions' mouths, so that they have not hurt me, because I was found innocent before Him; and also, O king, I have done no wrong before you."

Shadrach, Meshach and Abed-Nego

When they were commanded to worship the king, they refused even if it meant their death. But notice in their words, they were believing God to deliver them.

Daniel 3:16-18,20-26 Shadrach, Meshach, and Abed-Nego answered and said to the king, "O Nebuchadnezzar, we have no need to answer you in this matter.

➤ *Gift of Faith*

"If that is the case, our God whom we serve is able to deliver us from the burning fiery furnace, and He will deliver us from your hand, O king.

➤ *Total Commitment*

"But if not, let it be known to you, O king, that we do not serve your gods, nor will we worship the gold image which you have set up."

And he commanded certain mighty men of valor who were in his army to bind Shadrach, Meshach, and Abed-Nego, and cast them into the burning fiery furnace. Then these men were bound in their coats, their trousers, their turbans, and their other garments, and were cast into the midst of the burning fiery furnace.

Therefore, because the king's command was urgent, and the furnace exceedingly hot, the flame of the fire killed those men who took up Shadrach, Meshach, and Abed-Nego. And these three men, Shadrach, Meshach, and Abed-Nego, fell down bound into the midst of the burning fiery furnace.

➤ *God with Them!*

Then King Nebuchadnezzar was astonished; and he rose in haste and spoke, saying to his counselors, "Did we not cast three men bound into the midst of the fire?"

They answered and said to the king, "True, O king."

"Look!" he answered, "I see four men loose, walking in the midst of the fire; and they are not hurt, and the form of the fourth is like the Son of God." Then Nebuchadnezzar went near the mouth of the burning fiery furnace and spoke, saying, "Shadrach, Meshach, and Abed-Nego, servants of the Most High God, come out, and come here."

Then Shadrach, Meshach, and Abed-Nego came from the midst of the fire.

GIFT OF FAITH IN OPERATION TODAY

The gift of faith is given to the body of Christ for many reasons. As we learn to operate in it we will be used by God for the protection of ourselves, those around us and the body of Christ.

Without faith, it's impossible to please God.

With faith, nothing is impossible because when the gift of faith is operating, God's power for miracles will be released.

We begin by exercising our own faith. When we come to the end of that faith, very often, this special gift of faith will be released when God gives us a word of wisdom.

QUESTIONS FOR REVIEW

1. In your own words explain the power gifts. List all three.

2. What is the gift of faith?

3. Give an example from your own life of operating in the gift of faith, or give an example from the Bible in your own words.

Lesson Twelve

Power Gift

Working of Miracles

1 Corinthians 12:9-11 ... to another faith by the same Spirit, to another gifts of healing by that one Spirit, to another miraculous powers, to another prophecy, to another distinguishing between spirits, to another speaking in different kinds of tongues, and to still another the interpretation of tongues. All these are the work of one and the same Spirit, and he gives them to each one, just as he determines.

Nine Gifts of the Spirit		
Vocal Inspiration	**Revelation**	**Power**
Tongues	Distinguishing Between Spirits	Gift of Faith
Interpretation Of Tongues	Word of Knowledge	Gifts of Healing
Prophecy	Word of Wisdom	✏ **Working of Miracles**

WORKING OF MIRACLES

Definition

The working of miracles is a supernatural intervention in the ordinary course of nature.

It is a supernatural demonstration of the power of God by which the laws of nature are altered, suspended or controlled.

It is a gift of the Spirit given to the believer that he might work miracles.

The power gifts operate very closely with each other and with the revelation gifts.

How Gift Operates

The working of miracles begins with knowledge which has been received either naturally or supernaturally by the operation of the spiritual gift of the word of knowledge. Next, the spiritual gift of the word of wisdom is in operation. As this happens, we often see ourselves working a miracle before it happens. This "word of wisdom" releases the gift of faith. When that happens, we boldly begin to do what we saw ourselves doing by the word of wisdom.

It is called the working of miracles because we are an active participant in the miracle. What we see by a word of wisdom in the Spirit, we begin to boldly work out when the gift of faith is released. As we begin to operate in the working of miracles, God's power is released and the miracle happens. Thus, there is God's part and our part.

It's Easy

As this easy and quick progression of the gifts of the Holy Spirit operates, we find that it's just as easy to operate in the spiritual gift of the working of miracles as it is to give an interpretation of tongues, or to operate in any of the other nine gifts of the Spirit.

The key is to receive the revelation by receiving the word of wisdom.

Purpose of Miracles

The divine purposes for miracles can be:

> ➤ deliverance from danger
> ➤ protection
> ➤ providing for those in want
> ➤ carrying out judgment
> ➤ confirming the calling of a person
> ➤ confirming the Word which has been preached

The working of miracles will always bring glory to God and cause the faith of people to expand.

WORKING OF MIRACLES IN LIFE OF JESUS

There were no miracles recorded during the first thirty years of Jesus' life. He received the power of the Holy Spirit and after that the gift of working of miracles began to happen through His life.

First Miracle of Jesus

The very first supernatural manifestation in Jesus' ministry was a miracle. He interrupted the natural course of events and turned water into wine. He didn't turn grape juice into wine which would have been speeding up a normal process. He turned water into wine. That could never have happened without divine intervention.

➤ *Jesus Spoke – They Acted*

John 2:7-11 Jesus said to them, "Fill the waterpots with water." And they filled them up to the brim.

And He said to them, "Draw some out now, and take it to the master of the feast." And they took it.

When the master of the feast had tasted the water that was made wine, and did not know where it came from (but the servants who

had drawn the water knew), the master of the feast called the bridegroom. And he said to him, "Every man at the beginning sets out the good wine, and when the guests have well drunk, then that which is inferior; but you have kept the good wine until now."

➤ *The Result*

The disciples believed.

This beginning of signs Jesus did in Cana of Galilee, and manifested His glory; and His disciples believed in Him.

Feeding Four Thousand

Some of the miracles that Jesus performed were provision for the people.

Matthew 15:33-38 Then His disciples said to Him, "Where could we get enough bread in the wilderness to fill such a great multitude?"

Jesus said to them, "How many loaves do you have?"

And they said, "Seven, and a few little fish."

And He commanded the multitude to sit down on the ground. And He took the seven loaves and the fish and gave thanks, broke them and gave them to His disciples; and the disciples gave to the multitude. So they all ate and were filled, and they took up seven large baskets full of the fragments that were left. Now those who ate were four thousand men, besides women and children.

Testimonies Bring Faith

John 20:30,31 And truly Jesus did many other signs in the presence of His disciples, which are not written in this book; but these are written that you may believe that Jesus is the Christ, the Son of God, and that believing you may have life in His name.

EXAMPLES OF MIRACLES IN OLD TESTAMENT

Moses

Miracles were used to establish Moses' divine authority before Pharaoh.

➤ *Established Authority*

Exodus 7:9 When Pharaoh speaks to you, saying, 'Show a miracle for yourselves,' then you shall say to Aaron, 'Take your rod and cast it before Pharaoh, and let it become a serpent.'

Exodus 7:4,5 But Pharaoh will not heed you, so that I may lay My hand on Egypt and bring My armies and My people, the children of Israel, out of the land of Egypt by great judgments. And the Egyptians shall know that I am the LORD, when I stretch out My hand on Egypt and bring out the children of Israel from among them.

Elijah and Elisha

➤ *Elijah Parted Jordan*

2 Kings 2:8 Now Elijah took his mantle, rolled it up, and struck the water; and it was divided this way and that, so that the two of them crossed over on dry ground.

Elijah was established as a man of God and he walked in the miraculous much of the time. When it was time for him to go be with the Lord, Elisha was put to the test. When Elijah was caught up into the fiery chariot, Elisha was able to see into the spirit world and saw him go. Elisha didn't perform any miracles until after he saw Elijah taken up.

Then Elisha picked up the mantle of Elijah and came back to the River Jordan. Elijah had parted the river and they had crossed over earlier that day while fifty prophets looked on. What would Elisha do? Elisha had asked for a double portion of Elijah's spirit. The promise was, "if you see when I am taken from you, it will be yours." He had seen Elijah taken. Now, would he act in faith?

➤ *Elisha Parted Jordan*

2 Kings 2:13-15 He also took up the mantle of Elijah that had fallen from him, and went back and stood by the bank of the Jordan. Then he took the mantle of Elijah that had fallen from him, and struck the water, and said, "Where is the LORD God of Elijah?" And when he also had struck the water, it was divided this way and that; and Elisha crossed over.

Now when the sons of the prophets who were from Jericho saw him, they said, "The spirit of Elijah rests on Elisha." And they came to meet him, and bowed to the ground before him.

This miracle established Elisha as a prophet.

Axhead Swims

This miracle happened because of a need. One reason that we don't see more miracles is due to our own lack of belief. We reason that this or that isn't important enough for God's intervention. As we begin to step out in faith and expect God's gifts to operate in our lives, we will see the gift of the working of miracles in operation.

2 Kings 6:4-7 So he went with them. And when they came to the Jordan, they cut down trees. But as one was cutting down a tree, the iron ax head fell into the water; and he cried out and said, "Alas, master! For it was borrowed."

And the man of God said, "Where did it fall?" And he showed him the place. So he cut off a stick, and threw it in there; and he made the iron float. Therefore he said, "Pick it up for yourself." So he reached out his hand and took it.

Samson

Samson allowed himself to be bound by his own country-men and be delivered into the hands of the Philistines.

Judges 15:14,15 When he came to Lehi, the Philistines came shouting against him. Then the Spirit of the LORD came mightily upon him; and the ropes that were on his arms became like flax that is burned with fire, and his bonds broke loose from his hands. He found a fresh jawbone of a donkey, reached out his hand and took it, and killed a thousand men with it.

After this, Samson was thirsty and God performed another miracle just for him.

Judges 15:18,19a Then he became very thirsty; so he cried out to the LORD and said, "You have given this great deliverance by the hand of Your servant; and now shall I die of thirst and fall into the hand of the uncircumcised?"

So God split the hollow place that is in Lehi, and water came out, and he drank; and his spirit returned, and he revived. Therefore he called its name En Hakkore, which is in Lehi to this day.

If God was interested in satisfying the thirst of Samson, why wouldn't He be interested in taking care of our needs today? God desires to be involved with every area of our lives.

Samson didn't sound "super spiritual" when he told God of his need. But notice, he did tell God of his need.

BELIEVERS OPERATE IN MIRACLES IN GOSPELS

Walking on Water

When Jesus came walking on the water, the disciples were afraid.

Matthew 14:27-29 But immediately Jesus spoke to them, saying, "Be of good cheer! It is I; do not be afraid."

And Peter answered Him and said, "Lord, if it is You, command me to come to You on the water."

So He said, "Come." And when Peter had come down out of the boat, he walked on the water to go to Jesus.

If we are going to operate in the working of miracles, we must overcome our fear of failure and our fear of looking foolish. We must step out of the comfort zone of our traditions. Note that Peter first eagerly desired to walk in the supernatural gifts when he said, "command me to come to You on the water." Peter received the word of wisdom and the gift of faith when he heard the voice of Jesus saying, "Come!" Peter instantly obeyed, stepped out of his boat and began to operate in the working of miracles as he walked on the water.

Great Catch of Fish

Jesus said to Simon Peter,

Luke 5:4-7 "Launch out in to the deep and let down your nets for a catch."

And when they had done this, they caught a great number of fish, and their net was breaking. So they signaled to their partners in the other boat to come and help them. And they came and filled both the boats, so that they began to sink.

Jesus used this event to announce His purpose for the training of His disciples when he said, "I will make you fishers of men." Evangelism was at the heart of Jesus' ministry. If we are going to be effective in our ministries, no matter how foolish it may seem to us, we must be quick to obey the words of Jesus.

WORKING OF MIRACLES IN BOOK OF ACTS

Miracles Confirmed Word

Acts 8:5,6 Then Philip went down to the city of Samaria and preached Christ to them. And the multitudes with one accord heeded the things spoken by Philip, hearing and seeing the miracles which he did.

Miracle Power Promised

Acts 1:4,5 And being assembled together with them, He commanded them not to depart from Jerusalem, but to wait for the Promise of the Father, "which," He said, "you have heard from Me; for John truly baptized with water, but you shall be baptized with the Holy Spirit not many days from now."

Acts 1:8 "But you shall receive power when the Holy Spirit has come upon you; and you shall be witnesses to Me in Jerusalem, and in all Judea and Samaria, and to the end of the earth."

After Jesus had spoken His last words on this earth to His believers and had given them what we refer to as the Great Commission, Mark tells us,

Mark 16:20 And they went out and preached everywhere, the Lord working with them and confirming the word through the accompanying signs. Amen.

First Sermon

After the Holy Spirit fell on the day of Pentecost, Peter stood and delivered his first sermon. Signs and wonders were a part of that sermon.

Acts 2:22,43 Men of Israel, hear these words: Jesus of Nazareth, a Man attested by God to you by miracles, wonders, and signs which God did through Him in your midst, as you yourselves also know ...

Then fear came upon every soul, and many wonders and signs were done through the apostles.

WORKING OF MIRACLES FOR BELIEVERS TODAY

Miracles are to confirm the messenger and the message. How can we win a lost, sick, and dying world to a saving knowledge of Jesus without operating in the miraculous?

Hebrews 2:3,4 How shall we escape if we neglect so great a salvation, which at the first began to be spoken by the Lord, and was confirmed to us by those who heard Him, God also bearing witness both with signs and wonders, with various miracles, and gifts of the Holy Spirit, according to His own will?

Peter had fished all night without any results. Many times we, like Peter, try to operate according to our own knowledge. We should learn to say, "nevertheless, at your Word ..." We should take time to hear Him speak, to receive His Word through the revelation gifts of the discerning of spirits, the word of knowledge, the word of wisdom. Faith will come when we learn to be quick to obey and step out into the supernatural gift of the working of miracles.

Do Greater Works

John 14:12 Most assuredly, I say to you, he who believes in Me, the works that I do he will do also; and greater works than these he will do, because I go to My Father.

Why would Jesus say "greater works" if He didn't mean it? According to His words, we can do even "greater things" as the power of the Holy Spirit is manifested through the operation of the gifts of the Holy Spirit in our lives. God wants to continue to confirm His Word as the gift of the working of miracles is released to operate by our faith. God, not us, will receive all the glory.

QUESTIONS FOR REVIEW

1. Explain the working of miracles in your own words.

2. Explain the sequence of the other gifts of the Holy Spirit which usually operate in order to release the gift of the working of miracles.

3. Relate the personal miracle God did for Samson. Why is this important to you?

Power Gifts of Healing

1 Corinthians 12:9-11 ... to another faith by the same Spirit, to another gifts of healing by that one Spirit, to another miraculous powers, to another prophecy, to another distinguishing between spirits, to another speaking in different kinds of tongues, and to still another the interpretation of tongues. All these are the work of one and the same Spirit, and he gives them to each one, just as he determines.

Nine Gifts of the Spirit		
Vocal Inspiration	**Revelation**	**Power**
Tongues	Distinguishing Between Spirits	Gift of Faith
Interpretation Of Tongues	Word of Knowledge	✍ **Gifts of Healing**
Prophecy	Word of Wisdom	Working of Miracles

GIFTS OF HEALING

Definition

The gifts of healing are the supernatural impartations of God's healing power into people who need healing.

They are described as gifts (plural) because there are many ways to impart, or minister healing to the sick. They are described as gifts (plural) because many of the other nine gifts of the Holy Spirit are actively involved as we minister healing to the sick. The gifts are also spoken of in the plural since there are many ways to impart, or minister healing to the sick.

They are supernatural manifestations of the Holy Spirit and aren't the same as medical science.

Gifts in Action

The gifts of healing aren't a special endowment upon a certain believer, or his ministry. They are God's gift to the body of Christ and in particular to the one needing the healing.

These gifts can operate through any Spirit-filled believer.

All believers are to operate in these gifts when they do the works of Jesus and as they, like Jesus, are anointed by the Holy Spirit.

Healing and Gifts of Spirit

God has given His church nine different spiritual gifts. Several of these gifts relate directly to healing the sick. We must all learn to minister in these gifts if we are to effectively minister healing to the sick.

HEALING AND THE WORD OF KNOWLEDGE

Definition

Do you remember the definition for the word of knowledge? It is a supernatural revelation by the Holy Spirit of certain facts, present or past, about a person or situation, which were not learned through the natural mind.

Often in ministering healing, God will reveal a word of knowledge about a specific sickness which He wants to heal.

Sometimes it's for one specific person, and sometimes for a number of people.

Comes Through

The word of knowledge comes in different ways while ministering healing.

➢ *Feeling*

It may come through a feeling of discomfort in that particular part of the body of the one ministering.

This discomfort is often described like a pressure, a tingling, or a sensation.

It may be felt as a slight pain.

➢ *Word or Thought*

The word of knowledge can be by a word, or thought, which describes the sickness, disease, or pain.

This can be the name of the disease or the name of the part of the body affected.

➢ *Vision*

It can also come by a vision of the part of the body needing healing.

➢ *Location*

Sometimes, God will reveal the location of the person, or even the exact person which He desires to heal at that time.

This is occasionally described as a pull (as if by a magnet) toward that section of the room, to a particular aisle, or to the exact location of the person.

Other times, this can come as a light, or glow, or other feeling in the Holy Spirit which draws your attention to a particular person.

The Lord may reveal the name of the person, or other identification, which when spoken out will assure that person that they are the one whom the Holy Spirit is pointing out for that particular healing.

Faith Released

When the Holy Spirit reveals through the word of knowledge that He is going to heal a certain disease or a certain person, faith is released. Sometimes it's the gift of faith. Often the word of knowledge also releases the power gift of healing.

What God reveals, He heals!!

HEALING AND WORD OF WISDOM

The gift of the word of wisdom is a supernatural impartation of God's wisdom which reveals how we are to proceed on a course of action that will effectively minister to a certain need. It gives us the wisdom to know what to do with the knowledge that we have already received either naturally or supernaturally. It reveals how we are to minister to a need according to God's plan and purpose.

It is important that we take time to hear and see the Father's will so we will know if, who, when, where, and how He wants us to minister to a need.

John 8:28 Then Jesus said to them, "When you lift up the Son of Man, then you will know that I am He, and that I do nothing of Myself; but as My Father taught Me, I speak these things."

John 14:10 Do you not believe that I am in the Father, and the Father in Me? The works that I speak to you I do not speak on My own authority; but the Father who dwells in Me does the works.

Through the word of wisdom, Jesus was led to a certain man at the pool of Bethesda, and ministered healing in a different way. He healed many people in many different ways. He laid hands on them, He put His finger in their ears, He spit and touched their tongue, He cast out the spirits, He even healed by speaking only.

In Healing Ministry of Paul

Paul also ministered healing in many different ways as he was led to do so by the operation of the word of knowledge. Paul ministered healing through the laying on of hands and through handkerchiefs and aprons being taken from his hands and laid on the sick. Paul raised the young man, Eutychus, from the dead by falling on top of him and embracing him.

Before Paul ministered to the father of Publius, he prayed first, (apparently to receive a word of wisdom on how to minister healing to this man) and then he laid hands on him and healed him.

Acts 28:8 And it happened that the father of Publius lay sick of a fever and dysentery. Paul went in to him and prayed, and he laid his hands on him and healed him.

By the word of wisdom we may see ourselves ministering healing to that person in an unexpected manner. As this happens, often the gift of faith begins to operate and we simply do what God has revealed. When this happens, the manifestation of the healing always comes.

HEALING AND DISTINGUISHING BETWEEN SPIRITS

Spirits of Infirmity

The distinguishing between spirits is a supernatural insight into the spirit world. It shows the spirit, or spirits, behind a situation, an action or a message.

Often demon spirits of infirmity are responsible for a person's sickness, or disease. For example, there are spirits of cancer, arthritis, resentment, and bitterness.

By the distinguishing between spirits, the Holy Spirit will reveal, or put His finger on the exact source of the problem and the person can be delivered and healed.

Luke 11:20 But if I cast out demons with the finger of God, surely the kingdom of God has come upon you.

How Gift Operates

When a person is led by the Spirit of God, the manifestations of the gift of the distinguishing between spirits will come by an impression, or a thought, which reveals the name of the spirit of infirmity that is the source of the problem.

Cast out the spirit in the name of Jesus and the person will be healed.

Matthew 9:32,33 As they went out, behold, they brought to Him a man, mute and demon-possessed. And when the demon was cast out, the mute spoke. And the multitudes marveled, saying, "It was never seen like this in Israel!"

HEALING – GIFT OF FAITH – WORKING OF MIRACLES

Gift of Faith

➤ *Comes Supernaturally*

The gift of faith is a supernatural faith for a specific time and purpose. It is a gift of power to accomplish a certain task in whatever situation you are in at that particular time.

Sometimes, when faced with the need for a creative miracle or when ministering to a person whose need for healing requires a higher level of faith than where our faith has grown, God will supernaturally give us a special faith, so that no matter how impossible it may seem to man we know without a doubt that there will be a total manifestation of the healing.

Sometimes, people come to us who have part of their bodies missing through birth defects, surgeries, or accidents. Perhaps our faith has not gown to the point where we can believe God for the needed miracle. However, through a word of wisdom, we may have a vision and see ourselves ministering boldly in a certain way with the creative miracle taking place before it happens.

When we receive this word of wisdom through a vision, the gift of faith is released and we know without a doubt that the miracle will happen as we minister even as we have already seen it happening in the spirit.

➤ *Gift of Faith in Action*

Peter and John received a gift of faith the day they saw the lame man beside the temple gate.

Acts 3:6 ... Silver and gold I do not have, but what I do have I give you: in the name of Jesus Christ of Nazareth, rise up and walk.

Working of Miracles

The words of knowledge and wisdom release the working of miracles. Having received a word of knowledge, we have seen in the spirit by a vision or impression - a miracle happening before we have begun to minister healing to a person who needs a creative miracle of healing.

At that instant, we received a gift of faith. It is no longer a struggle to believe. We know without a doubt that as we minister healing the way we have already seen it happening, the miracle will occur. We boldly begin to operate in the gift of the working of miracles.

Mark 3:3,5b Then He said to the man who had the withered hand, "Step forward." He said to the man, "Stretch out your hand." And he stretched it out, and his hand was restored as whole as the other.

GIFTS OPERATE TOGETHER

As we have discovered, it's really impossible to say that this or that incident recorded in the scriptures happened through this gift or that gift.

The reason is simple.

The gifts of the Holy Spirit are manifestations of one Holy Spirit. They are so intertwined it's often impossible to separate them.

Sometimes the gifts operate together in one person, or two, or sometimes in a whole group. The beautiful reassurance we have is that whatever gift is needed, it is available to us!

As we boldly act upon what God has revealed, the healing is always manifested.

DOES ONE PERSON HAVE ONE GIFT?

No!

Does one person have the gift of faith, another the gift of miracles, and another the gifts of healing?

The person, or people, who need to receive the benefit of the ministry are the one ones who are to receive the gift from God through the operation of the gifts of the Holy Spirit. Instead of saying, "I have this gift or that one!" It is better to understand the gifts of the Holy Spirit and be ready to minister to others at any time in any one or all of the nine gifts of the Holy Spirit.

Develop "Faith Muscles"

If a person is baptized in the Holy Spirit, he has available to him all the gifts of the Spirit. But through false teaching or sin in his own life, he may have stopped or hindered the complete flowing of the Holy Spirit through him.

As he begins to exercise his privilege of operating in the manifestations of the Holy Spirit, they will grow in his life.

We sometimes say, "That person really operates in the gift of healing." And then we begin to think, "They have the gift of healing." (With the counter thought "I don't have that gift.") "I'll have them pray for me."

The truth is they have exercised their faith and moved in that particular gift more than you and so their "spiritual muscles" are stronger in that area.

In Public

When the body of Christ comes together and the gifts of the Spirit are allowed to operate, one will be given a gift of tongues and another the interpretation, or one will be given a prophecy and another a revelation gift.

God will divide the gifts between the body so that all may flow together. But the person who has exercised his faith in the area of giving prophecies will probably move in prophecy quicker. Thus, again we start to think, "Oh, he has the gift of prophecy. (I don't have the gift of prophecy.)"

Remember, all the gifts of the Holy Spirit can and will operate through every believer who has been baptized in the Holy Spirit and who will allow the Holy Spirit to minister.

In Conclusion

2 Timothy 1:6 Therefore I remind you to stir up the gift of God which is in you through the laying on of my hands.

Often there is an impartation, or a release, of the operation of the gifts of the Holy Spirit by the laying on of hands. Find an anointed minister, or believer, who operates freely in the gifts of the Holy Spirit. Ask them to lay their hands on you and release these gifts to operate freely in your life and ministry.

Paul wrote,

Roman 1:11 For I long to see you, that I may impart to you some spiritual gift, so that you may be established.

The gifts of the Holy Spirit are important ministry tools to build up the whole body of Christ and for evangelism.

➤ Continually keep these gifts "stirred up."

➤ Do not let them slip away.

➤ Expect them to operate in your life.

➤ Release them, daily, by faith into their full and accurate manifestation.

QUESTIONS FOR REVIEW

1. What are the gifts of healing? Why is it called "gifts," plural, when all the other gifts are singular?

2. How does the gift of the word of knowledge operate with the gifts of healing?

3. Which gift of the Spirit has God chosen for you? The answer is all! Now, write a list of the gifts of the Spirit you have operated in at least once.

4. What gifts of the Holy Spirit do you need to "stir up" in your own life?

Courses in This Series
By A.L. and Joyce Gill

The Authority of the Believer — *How to Quit Losing and Start Winning*

This life-changing study reveals God's provision for mankind's victory and dominion over Satan in the world today. God's eternal purpose for every believer was revealed at creation when God said, "Let them have dominion!" You will be released into a powerful new spirit of boldness as you discover how you can start winning in every struggle of life.

God's Provision for Healing — *Receiving and Ministering God's Healing Power*

This powerful teaching lays a solid Word foundation which releases the faith of the students to receive their own healing, walk in perfect health, and boldly minister healing to others. Many are healed as this revelation comes alive in their spirits.

Supernatural Living — *Through the Gifts of the Holy Spirit*

Every believer can be released into operating in all nine gifts of the Holy Spirit in their daily lives. From an intimate relationship with the Holy Spirit, each person will discover the joy of walking in the supernatural as the vocal, revelation, and power gifts are released.

Patterns for Living — *From the Old Testament*

God never changes! The way He deals with His people has been revealed throughout the Bible. What He did for His people in the Old Testament, He will do for His people today! You can learn the Old Testament truths to help you understand the New Testament.

Praise and Worship — *Becoming Worshipers of God*

Discover the joy of moving into God's presence and releasing your spirit in all of the powerful, fresh, biblical expressions of high praise and intimate worship to God. As you study God's plan for praise and worship, you will become a daily worshiper of God.

The Church Triumphant — *Through the Book of Acts*

Jesus announced, "I will build my Church and the gates of hell will not prevail against it." This thrilling, topical study of the book of Acts reveals that church in action as a pattern for our lives and ministries today. It will inspire us into a new and greater dimension of supernatural living as signs, wonders, and miracles are released in our daily lives.

The Ministry Gifts — *Apostles, Prophets, Evangelists, Pastors, Teachers*

Jesus gave gifts to men! These precious and important gifts are men and women God has called as His Apostles, Prophets, Evangelists, Pastors, and Teachers. Discover how these gifts are being restored to His Church, and how they function to equip the saints for the work of the ministry.

New Creation Image — *Knowing Who You Are in Christ*

This life-changing revelation will free believers from feelings of guilt, condemnation, unworthiness, inferiority and inadequacy, to be conformed to the image of Christ. It will release each believer to enjoy being, doing, and having all for which they were created in God's image.

Miracle Evangelism — *God's Plan to Reach the World* — *By John Ezekiel*

A powerful study which will release believers into becoming daily soul winners in the great end-time harvest through miracle evangelism. Like the believers in the book of Acts, we can experience the joy of reaching the lost as God confirms His Word through signs, wonders, and healing miracles.

Many of the manuals are available in other languages.
French, Korean, Russian, and Spanish.
There are also teaching tapes and videos that go with most of the courses.
Call Powerhouse Publishing for more information.
1-800-366-3119